NEW POEMS

1975

THE P.E.N. ANTHOLOGIES
OF CONTEMPORARY POETRY
already published by Hutchinson of London

NEW POEMS 1960
Edited by Anthony Cronin, Jon Silkin, Terence Tiller
with a Foreword by Alan Pryce-Jones

NEW POEMS 1961
Edited by William Plomer, Anthony Thwaite, Hilary Corke
with an Introduction by the Editors

NEW POEMS 1962
Edited by Patricia Beer, Ted Hughes, Vernon Scannell
with an Introduction by the Editors

NEW POEMS 1963
Edited by Lawrence Durrell
with an Introduction by the Editor

NEW POEMS 1965
Edited by C. V. Wedgwood
with an Introduction by the Editor

NEW POEMS 1967
Edited by Harold Pinter, John Fuller, Peter Redgrove
with an Introduction by the Editors

NEW POEMS 1970-71
Edited by Alan Brownjohn, Seamus Heaney, Jon Stallworthy
with an Introduction by the Editors

NEW POEMS 1971-72
Edited by Peter Porter
with an Introduction by the Editor

NEW POEMS 1972-73
Edited by Douglas Dunn
with an Introduction by the Editor

NEW POEMS 1973-74
Edited by Stewart Conn
with an Introduction by the Editor

NEW POEMS
1975

A P.E.N. Anthology
of Contemporary Poetry

Edited by
PATRICIA BEER

HUTCHINSON OF LONDON

Hutchinson & Co (Publishers) Ltd
3 Fitzroy Square, London W1

London Melbourne Sydney Auckland
Wellington Johannesburg and agencies
throughout the world

First published 1975
© P.E.N. 1975

Set in Monotype Garamond
Printed in Great Britain by The Anchor Press Ltd
and bound by Wm Brendon & Son Ltd
both of Tiptree, Essex

ISBN 0 09 125530 9

ACKNOWLEDGEMENTS

Acknowledgement is gratefully made to the poets who have allowed their work to be included in this anthology, and to the following publications: *Agenda, Aquarius, Boston University Journal, Chicago Review, Encounter, Hudson Review, Limestone, Listener, Little Word Machine, London Magazine, Matrix, New Review, New Statesman, Observer, Outposts, Oyez Review, Chicago, Poetry Book Society Christmas Supplement 1974, Poetry Dimension, Pembroke Magazine, Poetry Nation, Poetry Now, Poetry Review, Poetry Wales, Stand, The Times Literary Supplement;* and to Radio 3, Scottish BBC and Stroud Poetry Festival.

The poem 'Vipers' by Ted Walker appeared originally in the *New Yorker,* © 1974, The New Yorker Magazine, Inc.

CONTENTS

INTRODUCTION

There is no need to define at any length the criterion according to which I have selected these poems. It is precisely what anybody might suppose: I have chosen poems which I have admired and enjoyed and which I hope others will enjoy too. I think that the range of style and subject matter is sufficiently wide for many readers to find something to their taste. As in the case of the last three P.E.N. anthologies, the poems have been mostly taken from journals and magazines, though some, as yet unpublished, I have met at poetry readings and in the course of judging competitions. Poetry competitions in particular have brought to light very interesting work.

In one respect I have departed from accepted procedure. This time the poems are not arranged alphabetically under their writers' names. When I had assembled the material I wanted, I felt a growing conviction that certain poems positively demanded to be placed beside certain other poems, in order that both might gain from the juxtaposition. I have never felt A call to B or Y to Z in this way. So I took the step of arranging the work thematically, but not in any rigid sense. Sometimes the themes could hardly be paraphrased, but I feel, and I hope readers will feel too, that there is a movement or a rhythm in the collection which the alphabet does not provide.

I should like the first poem in the book, Gavin Ewart's 'Poets', to serve also as its epigraph.

PATRICIA BEER

NEW POEMS
1975

Gavin Ewart

POETS

It isn't a very big cake,
some of us won't get a slice,
and that, make no mistake,
can make us not very nice
to one and all – or another
poetical sister or brother.

We all want total praise
for every word we write,
not for a singular phrase;
we're ready to turn and bite
the thick malicious reviewers,
our hated and feared pursuers.

We feel a sad neglect
when people don't buy our books;
it isn't what we expect
and gives rise to dirty looks
at a public whose addiction
is mainly romantic fiction.

We think there's something wrong
with poets that readers *read*,
disdaining our soulful song
for some pretentious screed
or poems pure and simple
as beauty's deluding dimple.

We can't imagine how
portentous nonsense by A
is loved like a sacred cow,
while dons are carried away
by B's more rustic stanzas
and C's banal bonanzas.

We have our minority view
and a sort of trust in Time;
meanwhile in this human zoo
we wander free, or rhyme,
our admirers not very many –
lucky, perhaps, to have any.

Anthony Thwaite

ESSAYS IN CRITICISM

I like this more than that.
That is better than this.
This means this and that.
That is what this one wrote.
This is not that at all.
This is no good at all.
Some prefer this to that
But frankly this is old hat.
That is what Thissites call
Inferior this, and yet
I hope I have shown you all
That that way lies a brick wall
Where even to say 'Yes, but . . .'
Confuses the this with the that.

Instead, we must ask 'What is this?'
Then, 'Is that *that* sort of this,
Or a modified this, or a miss
As good as a mile, or a style
Adopted by that for this
To demonstrate thisness to those
Who expect a that-inclined prose
Always from this one – a stock
Response from readers like these.'
But of course the whole thing's a trick
To make you place *them* among those
Who only follow their nose,
Who are caught on the this/that spike
But who think they know what they like.

David Wright

WORDS

Often, when I go walking,
And the dialogue resumes, the
Interior gossip which has been
Going on since identity,

I've wished to put in a poem
Those illuminations, percepts
– What percepts! But in this art one may
Only be spoken through, although

At the same time I am saying
What only I can say. Older
Than we are, words and the language
Select our valid obsessions.

Constructing from words the poem,
I say what they say I should say
Rather than what I would say. They
Use us where we would use them.

The syntactical artefact
Implicit in its material
Like sculpture. Thus like a sculptor
One obeys the wood or marble

And, while shaping, collaborates
With a form that desires itself:
Till the unlooked-for for which one
Looked asserts a perfection.

Words, language: they have their eyes on
The unborn. Their order proceeds
From the dead but not yet done with.
Thus, when I fiddle with them, I

Meddle with matter existing
In other, further dimensions.
The poet is detached from the poem
With which he had something to do.

W. S. Graham

SGURR NA GILLEAN MACLEOD
(For the Makar & Childer)

Dear Makar Norman, here's a letter
Riming nearly to the Scots bone.
I rime it for it helps the thought
To sail across and makes the thought
   Into your Leod heid fly.
I thought I saw your words going
   Over the sea to Skye.

Here I speak from the first of light
On Loch Coruisk's crying shore.
Each bare foot prints the oystercatching
Sand and the ebb is cold streaming
   Itself and creatures by
Between my whole ten toes singing
   Over the sea to Skye.

Norman, you could probably make
This poem better than I can.
Except you are not here. Roll up
Your trews and let the old loch lap
   Your shanks of Poetry.
The bladder-wrack is smelling us
   Over the sea to Skye.

Maybe it doesn't matter what
The poem is doing on its own.
But yet I am the man who rows
This light skiff of words across
   Silence's far cry.
Don't be misled by rime. I row you
   Over the sea to Skye.

Norman, Skye, Norman I shout
Across the early morning loch.
Can you hear me from where I am?
Out on the shining Gaelic calm
    I hear your three names fly.
Look. It is the birds of Macleod
    Over the sea to Skye.

I row. I dip my waterbright blades
Into the loch and into silence
And pull and feather my oars and bright
Beads of the used water of light
    Drip off astern to die
And mix with the little whirling pools
    Over the sea to Skye.

And I am rowing the three of you
Far out now. Norman and Skye
And Norman keep the good skiff trim.
Don't look back where we are going from.
    Sailing these words we fly
Out into the ghost-waved open sea
    Over the sea to Skye.

Roy Fuller

VARIATIONS
For John Lehmann

According to a *TLS* review
Franck 'led an uneventful life . . . was not . . .
Prolific'. Might have been describing me.

The window frames a leggy yellow rose.
I hurry out to rescue drowning bees.
The bedside notebook yields its gibberish.

Franck: many boring bars; a schmaltzy tune;
Arguably, wit and singularity
Confined to the *Variations symphoniques*.

Not bad to be remembered even thus.
Each decade trendy geniuses arise;
Non-geniuses nearer to oblivion.

Ancients on benches, crumbling bread for birds –
It's they I should be with! Don't mind the young
Doing what's daring: I just want to think it.

The games of human love are infantile
Admittedly: my tragi-comedy
Is seeing them as puerile as well.

Making the relative allowances,
You're not, dear friend, as antique as your dog.
I can't yet pity you for walking slow

Or coughing when you rise to welcome me.
As for your fifty years' affair with iambs,
I envy it. No cause for faithlessness.

Creation seems continuous, looking back;
Yet we both know how random and how frail
The hours that make the opus numbers up.

I wish your study windows *cloches* for flowers . . .
More and more sweetness in your neighbours' hives . . .
Dreaming recalled and always metrical!

Douglas Dunn

STORIES

Once, once, O once upon a time –
I wish that's how a poem could begin,
And so begin one. That's how stories should.
The sweet parental voices started so,
Opening a book, *my* book, one given by
An aunt or such, inscribed 'for Christmas'.

No story ever did, I think, unless
Its author, sitting down, said, 'O I wish
That *this* is how a story could begin',
And so began, his tongue half in his cheek.
Once, once, O once upon a time –
It's real, magnanimous, and true! I wish,

And wish, and so my friends lose patience with
My stories, and they say, 'So this piece is
A story of lost gloves, and, yes, I know
I lost *my* gloves, but why this story, *this*,
This *making-up?*' *Once, once, O once upon*
A time, I say, You lost your gloves, and so . . .

Never, never, never, never, never . . .
That's a *good* line. And there was one which took
My senses to adventure on a day
Of wind and rain – 'One more step, Mr Hands,
And I'll blow your brains out!' Once, once, once, once . . .
I think the alphabet is tired of life.

'But be contemporary!' they shout, thumping
The table, and 'Yes, Yes,' I say, 'I'll buy
That, all or nothing. Just you wait, you'll see.
I'm of the times. . . . My pulse is topical,
And I love all the things I'm meant to love,
Am civil and 'sincere', one of the boys.'

Ah, that's better. I mean, I mean it *all*.
Yet when I start to write, my pen puts down
Once, once, O once upon a time . . . .
And that's for nothing and for no one,
Not anyone, not even for a child,
Who, at a table by a bowl of fruit

Sits down to read. It is too personal,
One sorry pass. I'll give away my thought
Of knowing that a life-discarded petal
Fell down, so slowly, when, a child, I read,
And landed on a page and was brushed off.
Once, once, O once, that happened so, like that –

Tender descent – and for a moment was
Completed by its image on the polished
Table. I took it in, did not forget.
Then, *am* I good? Was *that* benevolent?
Now, dignity of tables and of books,
What do *you* say? 'There is no answer, friend.'

Kit Wright

STORY TIME

A green oak stood
In bluebells reaching to the door
Of a toy house in a chocolate wood
Out of a children's picture book.

Look!
There in the house
By the oak in the bluebells
The old, old woman has fallen on to the floor

Out of her twisty bed.
I don't think she'll mend.
I think she's dead, don't you?
It hurt so much she didn't know what to do.

Towards the end
They cut a nerve in her brain,
Such the pain. Now, two things more,
Before you run out to play:

See if you can see
The children in the picture.
Then please say
Who the flowers are for.

Andrew Waterman

READING HABIT

At the end of each chapter, the end of the novel,
some of the characters are always left talking;
they drift out on a blank leaf,
paired or alone, down indeterminate vistas.

I put down the book. Leaves cry out
on autumnal boughs, are scythed by the driving wind helplessly,
the sky ebbs violet over the rooftops.
It is the close of another day,

and the lights that spring on show some characters still left talking,
framed in their windows a dinner party, a girl
brushing her hair, grey screens flickering
news of death picking off others, elsewhere.

So with 'good-nights' at doorsteps and bus-stops,
assuring 'until tomorrow', 'take care',
we float wrapped in coloured dreams out on a pure
white sheet, its comforting blankness.

Those who are no longer with us, the tyrant
cut down in an early chapter, the drowned fiancé,
the aunt who fought cancer meanly, must have been different,
there not for themselves, but for us to react to.

Not in my book, one saying
'He, by what he did, and left undone,
and how, and why, helps us shape our perspectives' –
the untrodden page still realizable before him.

Dannie Abse

UNCLE ISIDORE

When I observe a toothless ex-violinist,
with more hair than face, sprawled like Karl Marx
on a park seat or slumped, dead or asleep,
in the central heat of a public library,
I think of Uncle Isidore – smelly
schnorrer and lemon-tea bolshevik – my foreign
distant relative, not always distant.

Before Auschwitz, Treblinka, he seemed near,
those days of local pogroms, five year programmes,
until I heard him say, 'Master, Master
of the Universe, blessed be your name,
don't you know there's been no rain for years
and your people are thirsty? Have you no shame,
compassion? Don't you care at all?'

And fitting the violin to his beard
he bitterly asked me – no philosopher
but a mere boy – 'What difference between
the silence of God and the silence of men?'
Then, distant, as if in the land of Uz,
the answering sky let fall the beautiful
evening sound of thunder and of serious rain.

That was the first time Uncle went lame,
the first time the doctor came and quit hopelessly.
His right foot raised oddly to his left knee,
some notes wrong, all notes wild, unbalanced,
he played and he played not to that small child
who, big-eyed, listened – but to the Master
of the Universe, blessed be his name.

Isa Weidman

THAT FEELING'S WRONG

Slabbed in flowerless marble
grave, flowerily inscribed,
my Jewish father would have been
quietly miserable

at his two and only grandsons
marrying out – not so much
the faith – our irreverence
trained him well – as of the breed,
I don't suppose you'd call it race
in ethnological language;

Uneasily I also felt
more happiness is with your kind;
that feeling's wrong, and still I think
of oil with water, fish without
and in it lubbers drowning.

Donald Davie

FATHER, THE CAVALIER

I have a photograph here
  In California where
You never were, of yourself
  Riding a white horse. And
The horse and you are dead
  Years ago, although
Still you are more alive
  To me than any one living.

As for the horse: an ugly
  Wall-eyed brute, apparently
Tractable though, for I cannot
  Believe you were ever much
As a horseman. That all came late:
  Suddenly, in your forties,
Learning to ride! A surrogate
  Virility, perhaps . . .

For me to think so cannot
  Make you any more
Alive than you have been here,
  Open-necked cricket-shirt
And narrow head, behind
  The pricked ungainly ears
Of your white steed – all these
  Years, unnoticed mostly.

ROCKING-CHAIR

My wife's grandfather died in this rocking-chair.
This was his house. He built it. Only Kit Carson
reached this valley before him.

The chair squeaks. Not a sad sound. The living
and the dead can rock together sometimes and be
at ease. What's immortal of him

mellows the wood so the chair being empty is empty
specifically of him as though it had just stopped
rocking and could rock again.

Perhaps when he died he was admiring the Navajo
snowshoes on the wall. I'm sure even Kit Carson
abandoned this trail in Winter,

but the dead are narrower and pass easily
with their shadowy merchandise.

Navajos live in the desert and do not have snowshoes

Roger Garfitt

EN FAMILLE

They pass around the formal announcement of death,
for Papa chiefly, fresh from work. Almost two weeks
have passed since their cousin slipped, and only Madame
remarks, 'It might look somewhat better, borderless.'
The boys study the list of mourners, tracing uncles
and stray cousins, though one has strayed off the list.

DEATHBED OBSERVATION

Broken in my father's face,
The lock of anguish and dismay,
  And lines of laughter – burned away
  In death that turned his body grey.

Fell no dark upon that place.
Death relit a younger grace.
  Strange, in his own light he lay
  And he was handsome as the day.

George Tardios

PETROS

Aged Petros
And the mud wall
Supported each other.

Then
Heartcaught
By the log fire
Petros grew colder
Wood outlived rock.

Heartbeats ago
Limbs jerked
For nourishment.

They found him
Crumbling.
His glass of tea sat by
His side
Still breathing.

Outside
Mud dusted the ditch.

A REFUSAL TO MOURN
(*for Maurice Leitch*)

He lived in a small farmhouse
At the edge of a new estate.
The trim gardens crept
To his door, and car engines
Woke him before dawn
On dark winter mornings.

All day there was silence
In the bright house. The clock
Ticked on the kitchen shelf,
Cinders moved in the grate,
And a warm briar gurgled
When the old man talked to himself;

But the doorbell seldom rang
After the milkman went,
And if a coat-hanger
Knocked in an open wardrobe
That was a strange event
To be pondered on for hours

While the wind thrashed about
. In the back garden, raking
The roof of the hen-house,
And swept clouds and gulls
Eastwards over the lough
With its flap of tiny sails.

Once a week he would visit
An old shipyard crony,
Inching down to the road
And the blue country bus
To sit and watch sun-dappled
Branches whacking the windows

While the long evening shed
Weak light in his empty house,
On the photographs of his dead
Wife and their six children
And the Missions to Seamen angel
In flight above the bed.

'I'm not long for this world'
Said he on our last evening,
'I'll not last the winter',
And grinned, straining to hear
Whatever reply I made;
And died the following year.

In time the astringent rain
Of those parts will clean
The words from his gravestone
In the crowded cemetery
That overlooks the sea
And his name be mud once again

And his boilers lie like tombs
In the mud of the sea bed
Till the next ice age comes
And the earth he inherited
Is gone like Neanderthal Man
And no records remain.

But the secret bred in the bone
On the dawn strand survives
In other times and lives,
Persisting for the unborn
Like a claw-print in concrete
After the bird has flown.

WITH A WAVE OF HER OLD HAND . . .

With a wave of her old hand
She shut her past away,
Ninety years astray
In time's fading land,

With that dismissive gesture
Threw off pretence,
Rose to her proud stature,
Had done with world's ways,

Had done with words,
Closed her last written book
To ponder deeper themes
In unrecorded dreams.

John Ormond

AN ENDING

Lady, so long since gone, I am in limbo
Between an instinct of the dark, the sense
My own unfinished time has brought me to
And what you said you saw, and seemed to see,
On your last day. Feeling the faint pang
Of expensive appetite which, it appears,
Grates in the dying, you sent me running
For chicken and champagne. A whim, a delusion
Of hunger, that's all it was. When I returned
You saw things which I could not see.

Aren't the flowers dark? you said
Of the four yellow chrysanthemums which exploded
Pom-poms of formal light in silence
Under the black beams of that living-room
Turned sick-room; the ceiling the floor, too,
Of the empty room above in which you were born.

No one, I think now, could have invented
Such death-bed syllables. For then you said
(The poisoned, visionary words
Falling into the place of shining,
The chest of drawers, the cold brasses alive
At twitching firelight, the ticking clock
By the chimney stilled for your sleeping,
This place of much of your living
Which you had cleaned – how often? –
With cloth and polish and broom),
I can see dust on everything.

But far away you were gliding into a long beyond
Of snows, of future weather's total indifference,
Of your own uncaring. I held you in my arms
As you were dying, with no sense then of a need,
As now, which would ask, 'Why, where, these words
From one so prosaic, so afraid of any ending?'

Then you'd return with small apologies;
The sliced white chicken-breast unwanted,
The wine, in a kitchen cup to disguise
This once in a poor lifetime's last libation,
Spurned, too. Again, in shadows of shadows,
Which I believed you saw, you perceived not ease
But some uncounted-on and unaccountable
Glimpse of a pleasantness which made you say,
You who had been so afraid of your own eyes' closing
(Too easily persuaded, so I thought, of the goodness
Of this death – yet, was there someone there
Whose known gaze met your own?), *Well, well, well,*
What a surprise, what a surprise.

At last, in my arms still, those far snows
Finally kept you. The rituals done,
We stayed that night in the house together.
Neighbours fussed, grudgingly left us
Each with the other. I had no fear, mother.

And it was in my waking that I heard them,
My neighbours making up their morning fires
On either side. In the same world as them
I went down into the day that they and I would wear,
The winter sun's new garment. Into the room where you lay
I entered, took back the sheet from your face
And, without grief, grateful for your easy going,
Gave you the token of the love you were aware
No longer of, the kiss you could not share.

Forgive me for what happened then.
My lips upon your forehead tasted the foul grave
And I spat it to my hand and rushed
To wash the error from my proud flesh.

Isa Weidman

A WISH IN PASSING

Damned if I'll rest with arse sores
in an old people's place,
I'll get around doing
what I want, taunting fear

as long as
I'm no less conditioned
to being harmless;

then, or if I suffer,
they can treat me
to euthanasia,

a wish in passing.

Tom Lowenstein

THE DEATH OF MRS OWL

Mrs Owl lay grieving on the flat tarpaulin roof.
She propped her tired head on an old weathered piece of whale-bone.
The dog-team rested in a chained line behind the little house,
and howled in sympathy and hunger as she sorrowed.
'Alas,' she murmured, half aloud in the still air,
'perhaps I've kept my love-eye open for too long.
I see my future, as I do my past:
the dogs will bite my soft heart through and through.
This is my death-song, said the dying love-matron,
that I may finish with a pleasant epitaph:

   Let love and sunrise shut your eye,
   Rain from the half moon sweep the sky.
   Fear nothing when the eggs shall cry:
   Death shall not chill them though I die.

   But when your life is almost spent,
   Think of the kindness that I meant.
   Though you will love no more, do not repent
   I robbed you of your heart before I went.'

Uttering these words mournfully, Mrs Owl sank onto the roof,
one wing drooping over the whale-bone,
the other folded neatly into her stomach.
As the wind arrived to sweep away her spirit,
for one last moment, Mrs Owl shook out her feathers loosely
in a ruff of love; and with her big eyes still open,
staring at the empty sky, she fell asleep.
The north-east wind approached a little nearer,
and drifted over the tarpaulin,
lifting the spirit of Mrs Owl with gallant ceremony.
Out across the water swept the north wind, faster,
and soon the soul of Mrs Owl was cooing southward
on the Chukchi Sea across frozen waves
towards her sweet peninsula of change.

The dog-team got up stiffly from its frosty corners,
and stood stretching. Mrs Owl's remains lay quietly on the tarpaulin,
her snow-white feathers lifting pleasantly under the morning wind.

AFTER STEVENS

I

Today the mind is a part of the weather,
my shirt as red as the sun dying
between chimney-pots, and now
islands of cloud in a red sea beyond
the grey landmass invite the imagination.
I walked over to the typewriter
to put something down, a book
and a poem, but also that a poem
might catch the last five seconds of sun,
invitations specifically imagined. For now there is no red
and the brilliance of my shirt
is shining behind the landmass of all the clouds
of the mind.

II

Now it is the bulb, electricity: the sun
went so quickly and even with my back turned.
The world is dismal and the small pear tree
shaken as suddenly as sunset
by a bitter wind. I feel
the bitterness of the sight. I cannot feel
a man is tending
risen bulbs in all
good faith. Although he is
the wind must be making him think of the hearth, its
acrimonious consolation.

III
I used to swim out to the island
and head ecstatically for
the sun as it seemed
to lip the sea, cold fire
passing easily through water.
Yet its warmth was felt
long after as it is not now.
Remorseless at midday as it is not here.

C. H. Sisson

DROWNING

'With well-made songs, maintains th'alacrity
Of his free mind': or, as in my case, stutters
Eats out his heart at will, maintains friends
In expectation of loving, but does not love:
Twists words
Till they should have meaning, but they have none,
Kisses the earth, muddies his lips, and all this
Does not amount to a paid song, a footfall
Under the Almighty's feet, or a cool hand
Placed where I would place it, on the bare side
Of my shelled mistress, Anadyomene
Rising out of the sea in which I shall drown.

Molly Holden

FROM THE AMBULANCE

The weather is fine for those
outside, dry at least, the banked clouds
high and distant, the pavements
undarkened;

        but I see, tilted
to thirty degrees on the stretcher while
climbing hills, a view made menacing
by the russet glass. Beware.
The Malverns loom. There will be
floods, disasters, lightning, death.

But maybe only for us who travel
in county ambulances away from home.

C. H. Sisson

ONE EVENING

There are also bland days; they supervene
On fury and defeat
Open my side, see where the heart is

A smooth skin, traces of cool stone
But marvellous to the hand
What is there, Tertullian?

In my mind the roots quiver
Where will you touch, O root?
Mark this, the land set out.

But my mind is eaten by a strange fish
Chub or tench, stationary in the water
Only the lips moving.

John Hewish

FRIDAY EVENING, KENTISH TOWN
'Thoughts should clap hands, and say "Here we are".' – GOETHE
(According to Eckermann)

I know what he meant
This overcast evening in May,
End of an undemanding week,
Not a time to be idle.

Or to be content
With a toneless sky above Ken Wood,
Or the way the varied London brick
Of my neighbour's garden wall
(It bulged and was rebuilt)
In what comes through of afterglow
Is mildly fired again.

Or sup, as one who cannot sing.
These drives have cancelled out.
Between them, I cut my losses, watch
Dusk conventionally gather,
Darkening trees record
Weak currents of air.

Charles Tomlinson

INTO DISTANCE

Swift cloud
across still cloud
drifting east
so that the still
seems also on the move
the other way: a vast
opposition throughout the sky
and, as one stands
watching the separating
gauzes, greys, the eyes
wince dizzily away from them:
feeling for roots anew
one senses the strength
in planted legs, the pull
at neck, tilted
upwards to a blue that
ridding itself of all
its drift keeps now
only those few, still
island clouds to occupy
its oceanic spread
where a single, glinting plane
bound on and over
is spinning into distance and ahead
of its own sound

Molly Holden

IN THIS UNREMARKABLE ISLAND

We are always surprised by our weathers.

A morning sky is calm and apparently settled.
We assume a fine day to come. But clouds,
fine and soft, and ruffed like a comma's wings,
appear like phantoms in the distant blue.
We pay them little attention – perhaps they are
only signs of September at its best, a mellow sun
and the grass thicker with dew and shadow
than in these last few months.

                      But I
know what they mean; I am not surprised
by our weathers because I have had, perforce,
to sit and watch them change and come and go,
over the church or the chestnut, for nine years now.
I know the patterns of the sky and what they portend!
So now I watch a faint dappling in the west appear,
without surprise, and then (from nowhere apparently)
smooth pale banks of long and elegant cloud
behind those ragged wings that seemed diaphanous
at first but now become solid and significant.
I know that there will follow clouds scaled and veined,
and mares' tails twisted like ferns by winds at
incredible heights, and of incredibly cold
crystal, to such a coil of pattern
that no Celtic silversmith could match,
for all his skill. All this to herald rain!

Now, are we not spoilt, to live with such skies?
Although, soon after them, the sheet of faceless cloud
will move in on us from the west, drop,
silently drizzle, I would not live otherwhere.

They do not have such skies even in Calabria.

DOWNPOUR

A strong rain falls, a bony downpour.
The waters roar, like a riddance.
The day vanishes suddenly
and it is night that hesitates on a brink
for fear of difficulties. The rain, for instance.

Through the letter box, leaves instead of letters,
wet leaves blown along the path
and seeping through the low letter box,
an invasion that comes slowly,
but helped by the rain. The downpour.

I dream of thorns, aeroplanes and red horses,
but seldom of rain.
The creature spinning webs to catch its prey,
I dream of her too,
but almost never of rain. The webs of rain.

The rain does not slacken. It has the scent
of mistletoe. But it is a weapon, thrown.
The windows shine black with it.
I sit watching the knotted bunches of rain.
I do not want to cease watching. Such brawny rain.

But the dry house, its music and its meals,
recalls me from the window,
draws me back from a downpour that is drowning me.
I prepare to turn from the window,
yet remain a moment longer,
looking at the blur of the candle-flame
against the dark glass.

There is the downpour. Here is the uprush of light.

Eric Millward

SUDDEN RAIN

Leaving her work, she ran
Into the sudden rain
To linen long hung out,
To bring it in again;

But one sheet by the wind
Had been so fumbled and flapped
That when the pegs were taken
It still hung twisted and wrapped

And bound about the line,
And would not come to the hand
Of one who tussled and tugged
And could not understand

How often when we aim
To part or to divide
We find ourselves surprised
By knots we never tied.

AMITIES

Amities composed in gentle weather,
Flowering in temperate field or harbouring wood,
Or sealed at ease in warm and fragrant bed,

Flinch cravenly when winter swings his axe,
Raise hands in negative surrender when
Threatened by adversity's muscle-man.

It is the friendships built in bitter season,
When menace prowls the street and fields; when food
Is scarce and all you're left to share is need,

These are conjunctions nothing can unmake;
They will survive until all climates merge,
Proof against clock and calendar's furtive rage.

George Tardios

AUTUMN ROULETTE

Again
I risk
The fast road home.

A hedge-pheasant
Hedged between black trees
Blurs past.

Too long my mind's been set on black.
One summer long.

I spin my wheel
Into the red ferns
Skidding mud
And stop the clock.

The chameleon bird
I cannot see
Shows me –
The leaves have turned.

I. A. Richards

WINTER FLOWERING PRUNUS

Not a bee left on the wing,
Not even a fly
Blown by,
Not a bird yet come to sing
Or other glint of Spring.

This dauntless blossoming
Flings out its dawn-flushed snow,
Its gauntlet resolute
Defying TIME
For all who Him refute:
Usurper TIME,
Old Canceller, cancelled so.

This tree of trees,
Twirling and tossing in the gale
(Sheer emblem of His vagaries),
Here bequeaths,
With these wild wreaths,
To those whose hearts are now
Set on what TIME denies,
Their Everything.

Frail TIME.
As *was*, with *is* and *shall be*, dies,
Poor TIME:
Outwitted by a bough
Or rime.

Elizabeth Jennings

CELEBRATION OF WINTER

Any voice is soprano in this air,
Every star is seeding, every tree
Is a sign of belonging or being free,
Of being strong in the Winter atmosphere.
Nobody hesitates here.

There are sounds and there are spaces.
Human creatures could have left long ago,
Birds are migrants except
For an owl which woos and lullabies the night.
We are only waiting for snow.
The wind has swept away the brooding Summer,
Or has it taken flight?
Nostalgias are null. Eyes are a taper alight.

And winter reaches ahead, it stretches, it goes
Further than dark. A fountain is somewhere still.
What voice will come and fill
The emptiness of its no-longer overflows?
Any birth in Winter is hallowed by more
Than Advents or Bethlehems. The seas compose
Themselves perhaps for an Age of Ice, a shore
Where a child lifts a wave, where one gull chose
Not an inland cluster but broken wing and claw.
Any voice is sharpened upon this air
And if the sky sagged there would be more than one
    star to spare.

Peter Redgrove

PLAIN POEMS OF CHANGE IN FEBRUARY

One
Caesar died
The boy pared his nails
Rome fell
The boy crossed his legs
Pope Paul crumbled
Boy, we know you,
Give us parole.

Two
On Easter Day
I walked in the park
A window sun-flashed
I thought of a distant flat
And a woman writing.

Three
The long bones on the path
By the strenuous stream
Woke me with a start.
I had been travelling the winter
Merely pacing
Now I begin to run
She cannot be far away.

Four
Why at my age
Did I perch in that crotch?
Did that tree teach me to sing?
Did it teach me to slither?
Suddenly I had an audience
Three ladies mooning and a black policeman.

Five
There are inky fingermarks
In 'The London Shakespeare'
There is a trail of them
Through 'Exploring Poetry' and 'The Act of Creation'
There is a geological hammer
With an inky handle
And the typescript of a novel
In the green chair
The wedding-ring is in bed already
Snoring, the right road home
Printed across the books.

Six
The cat rubs his tom-bottom
On the mould under the thin leaves,
Last year's rose-leaves,
He prepares for Spring.
The first condition of the ghost
Is that it returns.

Seven
Deep in the found night
At the window of dreams
The thriving greenhouse
Of the lost day's orchids.

Eight
I like that wet lady in the muslin
Who catches fishes that can breathe water
And men who cannot.

Peter Scupham

LAND'S END

The Grand Bard's wreaths and rituals decay,
Those sky-blue robes, archaic lexicons.

His old house bleaches among shoals of hay,
Voyaging nowhere all the summer long,

Worked by a dynamo of sentenced bees
Lodged in a cave under our bedroom sill.

As yet, their tongue needs no revivalist;
The walls thrum to a doomed plainsong.

We grieve upon their notice of eviction
Whose hive will congregate no sweetness.

All tenancies, save one, are held on lease.
We claim our native element's forbearance,

Yet stony seas leech out a dying tanker:
Languages founder, Lyonesse goes down,

And the Bard lies under slate in Zennor churchyard
Whose fingers carved unsinkable trim ships.

Patricia Duncker

PALISADOES, JAMAICA

A long tenuous sliver, black man's land,
Curving round the harbour like my mother's arm.
Port Royal at the tip, sunken into the sea
By an earthquake, before I was born.
The road's the most important thing –
White wind-scattered sand and scrub brush
Sweeps over the asphalt that melts in the heat.
There's a new slabstone airport out there.
We, children, stared up at the heavy glazed jets,
And frightened, yet drawn to the danger,
Ran, prodding dead jelly-fish, all down the beach
Till we stopped, hanging fast to the high wire-mesh fence,
Just a slash of built steel across the waste.
There was a jetty where the ships tied up,
To take away cargoes of gypsum
From five white slate mountains half slithering into the sea.
I dressed myself up like a queen in the seaweed
And strode quite impressively into the dunes.
My mother was almost asleep and wouldn't say
Why the ships took the white rocks away.

THE SCENE OF THE CRIME

Time and again I've tried to picture it –
Verandah, the slapping boom of the canvas blind,
Sticky poinsettia sweat, the normal heat
Which piles up in the varnished rooms,
The sense of something always left behind,
When over the terrified child the wardrobe looms.

What happened here, I ask, as I walk round
The imagined space? A boy and then a man
Outwore an older man and one day found
That reticence is love: an accepted defeat
Lived on with a death, a pointless plan
Was worked out in an unimpressive street.

Soon I'll come home and open the white gate
And put my sophistication to the test;
Through travel, work and other love, my fate
Is looped to this first house of dreams;
These rooms and faces will at last find rest
When everything in me is what it seems.

John Cotton

MOORLAND SIGNALS

Behind the stone cottage
The wife pegs out her washing,
a bright bunting
of challenge to the grey
power of the moor
which, like the vasts
of a terrestrial sea, casts
up, from time to time,
a pony or a sheep.
Out of the mists and rime
such visitors stare at night
at the homing beacon
of the cottage's square of light.

Elaine Feinstein

BY THE CAM

Tonight I think this landscape could
   easily swallow me: I'm smothering
in marshland, wet leaves, brown
   creepers, puddled in
rain and mud, one little gulp and

I'll be gone without a splutter:
   into night, flood, November, rot and
river-scud. Scoopwheeled for drainage.
   And by winter, the fen will be brittle and
pure again, with only an odd, tough, red leaf frozen
out of its year in the ice of the gutter.

Peter Brennan

TWO FRAGMENTS
DAWN AND MORNING A28

How still it is the lorries only emphasize.
Through chinks
in the curtains
a strange light of an indistinct no-
colour peers and scrapes. Moving things
pass through it jaggedly risking
a coarse and dry sensation.
The birdsong
is still tuning up,
the lorries broadcast
longwaves alongside the muzak.
The thrush requires
specially adapted receivers.

The Dover ferry came in half-an
-hour ago. From Warsaw Hamburg Pa-
ris lorries
thunder down upon us.
Men eight feet off the ground
guide them. They have driven through many nights.
They have slept on coffee-stained
seats curled up like mangy cats and then
the boat docks as the engines shake it rigid as they falter
to a halt. Blur.
Disgust. And by the time they get here
they're just waking up. There are
two people in each of these worlds.
They speak the same language.
They argue
as do we as to just what those words may mean, Warsaw
Hamburg Pa-
ris. Laughs.

Kevin Crossley-Holland

CLEAN MONDAY, RAMNOUS

A fallen streamer rustles and sidles
Across the floor. After each guest and gust
The door slams; a youngest daughter bridles
At some strange hungry smile, and in the dust

Outside, the hens scatter at the clatter
To the rough yard's corners, nettles, the fence.
Their loss is that nothing does not matter:
Assiduous devotees of nonsense,

They peck at grit and small chips of marble
And ignore the field's red lips across the road
Where the man waits. The swirling winds garble
His shouts, translate them into ode, then goad.

His girl hears, rises; again the door slams.
He carries a kite – an eagle or buzzard.
With skill he hoists it, plays it, now it runs
And climbs further before blast and blizzard.

Then his daughter takes it. When it tugs, dives,
She shrieks with such excited fear, aware
Of ravening beyond her, and of lives
She could live that have not yet escaped her.

So she yields, he resumes. Hand over hand
He holds the line just as he grasps his spade.
This one day he abandons the land;
He forgets the vine, the growing green blade,

His taverna's patrons, already tight.
He is washing off the soil of the year,
Acknowledging Lachesis. The great kite
Is like a tongue preying on air, a prayer.

Henry Reed

BOCCA DI MAGRA

This must endure,
This which so dazzles us now, and flaunts itself,
Must soon endure
Silence upon the ecstatic shouting voices;
And the benign air chilled that strokes our bodies
Must endure,
Us absent, another December on the sand-dunes
And lonely wincing sunlight on an ice,
Which may form (it is known to have done so before)
On the harmless stream that now
Placidly greets the sea in blue to blue:
All this must endure
Winter.   So, God forgive me, must you.

You are poor, my love.

That colour on your cheeks and on your brow
Will blanch again, and the resistless print
Of the claws of the frost will mark them and mar them.
Your voice and mine will leave our joyful echoes
(Spinning, now spinning up into the lighted air)
To the damp absorption of the palisade,
And the pine and the willow-wood,
And emerge, us gone, as the fretful mouthings of winter,
Hoarse in the caverns, or simply muttering
In the damp and rotting constructions mouldering here.
And if from their grovelling slumber
A murmur swells, it will swell not with our warm voices,
But rise and shriek in a whirlwind of blinded crying,
Screaming along the river's bank to greet its companion,
The great impassive cold that already seems to chide us
From the bluffs of Carrara, gashed by the great into greatness.

                                        I, too, shall be poor, my love
In a different way. How foreign it is to think
This time next year, if there is a next, we may meet as might academics,
And compare the findings which I shall so much dread.
(Am I so loveless, my love, or only trustless?
No, I am neither, my love.) I shall gravely and bravely surmise
And hope that at this thin mouth of the estuary,
The blue to the blue returning,
I shall feel, as last year and this, your warm, good mouth beneath mine,
And see, unchanged,
The shy agreeing sweet suggestion in your eyes
As one of us murmurs: 'We know of places elsewhere.'

Peter Dale

SWIFTS

The swifts are back,
their flight on a knife-edge.
In the dusk we watch them
and feel at peace.
Their grace we take
as confirmation.

Our swifts are back,
we say, and touch now.
But their grace survives them,
whichever were ours.
And it hurts to touch you,
that wing of hair.

Whose love, my love
in my hands tonight?
Whose spring again
in the bounce of your hair?
Our love is ghosted;
our swifts return.

Laurence Lerner

THE BEECH IN THE PARK

I shiver, and turn yellow; fill the air
With spurts of tiny flame that burn to brown,
Let fall my leaves, and stand up naked in
A pool of brown.

And still the bipeds pass.
Each day they change their bark.
This is he, this is she:
All winter, restless.

She stares at me, and as the brown leaves hover,
Catches one, feels it tear,
Turning it over, brittle to her hand;
Crunches it, turns away.

One day saw him,
His branches drooping, staring at the grass,
Kick up my leaves with slow and slower steps.

One day saw her,
A red scar on her bark
And raindrops streaming, stumble through my leaves.

I shut my veins to keep the winter out;
Sleep standing, through the cold.
The bipeds drop to earth; their dark sap spills;
They lose their last remaining leaves; and stiffen.
Poor creatures, for whom wind and snow
Exist within as well; for whom
No spring will bring new leaves.

Kevin Crossley-Holland

PETAL AND STONE

An old antithesis: petal and stone.
There were anemones near that valley site,
Furled against such freezing wind. They alone
Looked living in that mottled place – blood-bright.

She dropped to her knees by a brilliant
Colony, carefully selected one,
And leaned back against a rock. That was all
It seemed, but it could have been a lion:

Only the torso, and that mauled by time,
But still the defiant cold lord of the land.
She stretched out against it, so tender, feline:
The flower had opened to wilt in her hand.

Georgina Hammick

THE PRISONER

The princess in the tower
Is waiting for her prince;
She will let down her hair
For him to advance.

He will arrive tonight
And stay in her arms till dawn.
She imagines how his weight
Will drag her head down.

She imagines how his weight
Will pin her to the bed
As the rats run over the floorboards
And the owls hoot overhead.

As the owls hoot in the rafters
And the rats run round the floor,
He will comfort her with kisses
And tell her he loves her more

Than the treasures of his kingdom,
Than his horses and his men –
Who parade every day before breakfast
On the emerald castle lawn.

The princess sits there dreaming
Of how her prince one day
Will rescue her from this prison
And gallop her far away

To the castle in the mountains
Where his horses and his men
Change guard every day at breakfast
And again in the afternoon.

For every time he visits
He brings a skein of silk,
And she's weaving it into a ladder
In the evenings after dark.

The princess stands there ready,
Tightening her rope of hair;
She does not know (as we do)
That the witch will climb the stair.

And because I, in my childhood,
Could hardly bear to look
At the wicked witch and her scissors
In the frightening fairy book

As she snicked the golden tresses
And jeered at the shaven head,
And then waited in a passion
To greet the prince instead –

I'll stop the projector whirring
And freeze the image. Here
Is a girl at the window watching –
About to let down her hair.

Thomas Blackburn

LUNA

Where is there an end to it the river of women,
Walking proudly through time on their high-heeled shoes,
On their shoulders for a space the weight of being human
The tale of their being here will never close.

They step into their births and put on sorrow
Like a purple vest a mantle of dark green
Then the bow is drawn, the string shoots forth the arrow
And they follow its course to a target that cannot be seen.

The sound of the music of their movement
Sweetens with praise the dull hammer blows of time
Through the intricate metres of their slow advancement,
God, through his daughters here, is taking aim.

And it unfolds the steel petals of the rose of their being
And scented like the rose in an expanding tense
They walk with light feet over the apotheosis of ruin
Obeying the far gone conductor of the intolerable dance.

Where is there an end to it, the river of women
Walking proudly through their dust through devious ways,
The high keen merriment of their passing
All that is not dust must continually praise.

Derwent May

WONDERING ABOUT . . .

Wondering about many women – all
Who looked at me and fell into my care;
Wondering about what they used to feel,
How much they laughed, how much they chose to bear;
Whether any sigh to think of me still,
If they fix a year by our affair.

Wondering about the one who by a kiss
Set all that was really meant in train,
Laid up for me and for herself
Strange shares of tenderness and pain,
And will not see another take her place
– As now she steps in through the door again.

THREE GIRLS

Faith had a fatherless child,
Something had been misplaced.

Charity saw good in everyone,
Until her eyes gave out.

Hope became a chorus girl,
She springs eternally.

Who is the greatest of these?
They are equal. They abide.

R. D. Lancaster

TO KAREN

When your grandchildren
In fifty or so years' time
Return from the Moon
To take A-Level English –
Candidates must sit for it

On their native Earth –
One will suddenly jump up
Out of the strange grass
With what you once called a book
With what you remember as

Poetry in it –
They may not have to wear clothes
Or get their hair cut
But most computered workers
Have to study Useless Arts;

You are, by this time,
You have to admit, awake
In your rocky chair
And ready to hear this pest
That's jumped up out of the grass.

'Granny, didn't you
Once tell us you went to school
In the town mentioned
In several of these poems?'
And you're shown the very lines

But your glasses fall
Into a basket of wool,
Antique ornament
You prize like Wedgwood vases
And useful in a crisis

Such as this; the drugs
Even these tiniest tots
Push on old Granny
To check if she tells the truth –
'Granny, here's your cup of tea.'

Then two others press
Moon-faces into your ears:
'Granny, isn't this
Your first name mentioned in this
And this and this and this one?'

Now you feel barren
Of any inspiration
To answer that one.
Then pet child whispers 'Haroun!'
For no apparent reason.

'Haroun-al-Raschid!' –
No doubt some place on the Moon –
So they run off to
Their Watership Down warren
To kill time while you're blushing,

Leave you to their text
So wide open in your lap
You see the reply
Now to what you once asked him:
'Born in 1922'.

A. McColm

MIDSUMMER EVE

Then, when you, more exciting
than any girl in a bar but not yet
loved openly, my dearest friend,
put the coins you had kept
warm from your hand to my hand
with your eyes and lips trembling
at last, I heard the latch click.

Hush, murmurs of rendezvous
in the garden – I know that gate
of smoothed, clumsy estate
timber, above the intake,
and through the drystone wall
to the bare fell.

To celebrate your beauty I pretend
the good time unattained;
not that we fear rank evil;
but that uncertainties attend.

Derwent May

COMING BACK

Hurrying – hanging back – along the street.
Light from the house lost in the yellow glare.
Light in the hall. A hand on the cold rail:
The palm tense. Silence on every stair.

Smiling faces in frames – taut and still.
A sigh begins to tremble in the air.
The air flies past. Black through an open door:
The silence of sleep! – and her dark head lying there.

Alan Brownjohn

THE SEVENTH KNIGHT AND THE GREEN CAT
A Variation on the Gawain Poet

Curious about her seven daughters, in turn came
The seven fortitudinous knights. And the first
To sit by the swarming fire, sipping mead with
Mother and eldest daughter, saw with much delight
The white cat pace to him, as he loved them,
Cats.
   The creature was unbleached to a queer
Shifting shade of green by the colours of the room
– Green hangings, green velvet on the couches,
Green branches at the window, green eyes in matron and girl,
Green even in the flames of the fire because
They cast salt in the crevices of the coals to
Make matching colours.
                So the white cat
Mewed at him, nudged his ankle, mounted his lap,
And the mother murmured, 'You are much honoured.
She has never before walked in such a way up to a man.'

This flattery went deep, the proposals were made, and the pair
Duly wed.
          And since daughters must dutifully marry,
And mothers must needs be mothers, and marry off,
A second knight came seeking the second daughter
And chose a green chair by the great fire while
The mother poured wine.
             Again, willingly, the white
Cat rose on her green cushion, stood stretching,
And patterned the flagstones to the handsome second knight
To form fond figures-of-eight round the man's thin legs.
'There's a something about you that attracts her, she
Has never lingered with any man,' the lady said.
In this style was her second daughter secured
To a cat-adoring knight.

This way it went too
With the third, the fourth, the fifth and the sixth, on
A succession of green days with the cat casually
Trusting its truly-said-to-be-so-untypical
Affection to the different knights, whether of
Aragon, Transylvania, Tartary or Tibet, being
Similar only in their peculiar pride at pre-empting,
Uniquely, an unsociable animal unsure of men:
Cat-lovers, but gullible with it, which is rare.

On the last and greenest day, green curtains gathered
Across the storm which sent the green branches seething
Over the sky in a frenzied trellis-work of green,
The seventh knight finally knocked; one who knew
And loved cats more than any of these lovers, and
He yearned for the youngest daughter's hand.

                                        Her mother
Decanted liquor as usual, and the lovely daughter sat,
And green flames flashed in the hearth as the cat
Began again, greenly, its meaningful trek of the floor.
'She will not go to you, she has never gone to greet a man',
The matron predicted; but the cat pounced all at once,
From no definable angle, onto the very codpiece of the doting
Knight, and neatly nestled.

                        So the mother and girl
Cried equally with eagerness and ecstasy as before

– At which the knight bounded up from his bench of green,
Shouting, 'I am getting out, out of here at once!'
And 'I know what sort of situation this is,'
Dropping the cat, flat-eared and snarling with dire dismay,
To the stones, decapitating the thing with a dirk;
With screams from all, except himself and the evil cat's
Head which jeered, and rejoined itself to the body
And said, 'What was that intended to imply?'
'The true friend of cats,' said the knight, 'knows
That cat in ninety-nine which walks for women
And not for itself alone, the animal which is
The familiar of witches.

But it seems as if
I have not exorcized this particular one enough.'

'You are remarkably right,' said the restructured cat
Sapiently, 'and for this wisdom you will wend,
By a promise you will here and now provide,
One year through numerous travails of the world and come
To the terrible temple of the cat-goddess,
The mere pictures of whom inflict fevers and death
On the temerous beholder who braves them, and
Leading lady of many a lousy psychotropic
Trance. There we shall truly meet again,
And I shall take my turn.'

          So the seventh knight
Ground on grimly over the bogs and crags of the world,
Lodging roughly, going rudely his slow way
On his bewildered horse through innumerable bleak,
Colourless, sleazy, subtopiate regions,
Demoralizing tracts of megalosuburbia,
And came, just after eleven heavy months, to a splendid
Castle, where he was welcomed very festively.
                    There,
In the course of after-dinner prattle of the price of property,
He thought he might try to elicit where the temple
Of the great cat-goddess stood, half-hoping it had not
Survived redevelopment.
            'My fine fellow, I can
Tell you the lie of the land,' said the lord his host,
But linger a day or two here, love, enjoy some relaxation'
– And his lady smiled in sly sympathy and accord –
'While I do some terribly tedious hunting. And, by the way,
Be good!'
          With an inward feeling of distant déjà vu,
The seventh knight agreed; and for three successive days,
Was allowed to lie lazily in his bed while his host
Hunted and left his lady behind (just as he had read
   somewhere:

Because, to truncate a tangled tale,
Coming in sleek, scarlet, delightful garments,
She insisted on sleeping with him thoroughly each of the three
Days her husband was out happily hunting the evening meal,
Which the knight acquiesced in with an uneasy sense of
Compromise and suspicion.)
                              Each night, the master
Hot and bothered, and scenting himself, brought back
The special spoils of a strenuous day in the field;
For this supper asking nothing in return and reward
But the knight's company in anecdotes and carousing;
And on the last day, as promised, he provided
Instructions for reaching the great cat-goddess' place.

It proved a daunting plod over muddy areas,
An extremely unclean excursion, so that when the knight
Arrived there, both he and his horse exhausted,
Spattered in the saddle from travel, he thought it was his
    tiredness
That stopped him from seeing where it was. But suddenly,
He saw it, a low brick thing nearly hidden in the grasses
Of a thistly field, with peculiar peep-holes from which
Any occupant, sitting in a safe nook, could
Scan out.
          Dismounting, the knight called, clearly, and
Loudly as he was able, on whoever lurked inside to
Emerge, and there expeditiously appeared a
Truly tremendous cat, the size of a full-grown woman.
'As I promised and pledged I would do, in all duty,'
Stated the knight, 'I have travelled to the temple
Of the great cat-goddess to pay the penalty for
Following up certain suspicions too rashly,
And acting in anger.'
                      The vast cat mysteriously smiled,
Saying, 'Listen. As an artful knight, you showed
Some shrewdness in discerning a witch's cat;
As a truly brave one you moved boldly
Against a defenceless, domestic beast; as
A plodder you showed some powerful persistence
In going your way through the world for a whole year

To find out this frightful place; as a seizer of chances,
You lay three times with the lady of the castle,
Obviously not having offered any oath you would thereby
Break; thus, a clean code of knightly
Tactics you have most tightly kept, and
Will be rightly rewarded.'
                              At which the vast animal
Cast off its outer cat-costume to step calmly
Forth as the seventh daughter, dressed in the delightful,
Scarlet, sleek garments of the mistress of the castle.

'I was,' she said, 'all the time secretly concealed
In the little anatomy of the cat, and in the body
Of the lady of the castle you came to know a bit,
And the knight of the castle, my master and lord,
Was all the time my own dear mother in drag.
So on the basis of all that you may bow, and beg now
The hand of the youngest daughter you came to collect.
There is no way out.'
                              So, haltingly heeding
These dreadful words, the dumbstruck fellow put
His proposals, too perplexed to do other, and the pair
Were rapidly wed. And they went on to work through
Many years of irrefrangible, retributive wedlock
(For she truly turned out termagant as well as witch).

– Yet concerning these travails, I cannot, truthfully, say
I am sad or sorry, and I cannot make this knight an
Object of pity; because as a grown-up I genuinely regard
Knights and knighthood and the weapons and mores
Of a warrior society as both juvenile and degrading.

Jenny Joseph

DAWN WALKERS

Anxious eyes loom down the damp-black streets –
Pale staring girls who are walking away hard
From beds where love went wrong or died or turned away,
Treading their misery beneath another day
Stamping to work into another morning.

In all our youths there must have been some time
When the cold dark has stiffened up the wind
But suddenly, like a sail stiffening with wind,
Carried the vessel on, stretching the ropes, glad of it.

But listen to this now: this I saw one morning.
I saw a young man running, for a bus I thought,
Needing to catch it on this murky morning
Dodging the people crowding to work or shopping early.
And all heads stopped and turned to see how he ran
To see would he make it, the beautiful strong young man.
Then I noticed a girl running after, calling out 'John'.
He must have left his sandwiches I thought.
But she screamed 'John wait'. He heard her and ran faster
Using his muscled legs and his studded boots.
We knew she'd never reach him. 'Listen to me, John.
Only once more,' she cried. 'For the last time, John, please
    wait, please listen.'

He gained the corner in a spurt and she
Sobbing and hopping with her red hair loose
(Made way for by the respectful audience)
Followed on after, but not to catch him now.
Only that there was nothing left to do.

The street closed in and went on with its day.
A worn old man standing in the heat from the baker's
Said 'Surely to God the bastard could have waited.'

John Cotton

LEICESTER SQUARE: MAY 1974

Will Shakespeare leans at ease,
his right arm on a pillar topped with books,
his stone cloak unruffled in the breeze,
as constantly across the square he looks,
where letters five feet high
announce Fitzgerald's *Gatsby*
and what we take to be
the eyes of Dr Eckleburg.
But these are brown not blue?
We look again
to find they are the two
enormous boobs of Jenny,
'a ride like you never had before',
the *Swinging Stewardess*
of the film that's shown next door;
and, as if to stress
the confusion of fantasies and themes,
and, still, a good wine needs no bush,
while *Gatsby* seems
to have no more than lettering,
Jenny's full-frontal dreams
are cut short at the hips.
Though Shakespeare always had it sorted in his head:
for the one a tragedy, for the other
the second best bed.

Pamela Lewis

EVERYTHING YOU EVER WANTED
TO KNOW . . .

I like my children's friends.
It's their parents that worry me,
we play smooth games of civility with them,
it's a variety of bridge.
We meet them indoors and outdoors,
at games fields and around the edges
of parties and dates.
Coca Cola conversation
caught across corners interests me;
I offer crisps and empathy.
'My Dad burnt my Penthouse.'
'You can't tell my Mum
I saw Woody Allen at the cinema
being funny about sex, I told her
we went bowling.'
What do their Dads do
to their Mums or sidekicks
that they have to pretend
that at sixteen you sit on
doll bottoms of pink inviolable plastic?
Posh Dads who wear cavalry twill
and twitch, and Mums who hoot
under sheepskin and headscarves
at the ball games,
I hope you don't notice
that I observe you sideways.
Your children I meet full frontal.

Fleur Adcock

THINGS

There are worse things than having behaved foolishly in public.
There are worse things than these miniature betrayals,
committed or endured or suspected; there are worse things
than not being able to sleep for thinking about them.
It is 5 a.m. All the worse things come stalking in
and stand icily about the bed looking worse and worse and worse.

Pat Arrowsmith

PRISON REFORM

In the bad old days
no watches were permitted.
We did our time
not knowing what the time was.

Now watches are allowed
we have the satisfaction
of knowing how slowly
the time passes.

Penelope Shuttle

GHOST

Ghost:
A state of being shaken,
cold vibration, trembling fields,
shadows of snow

My ghost:
whose smile resembles soft slate,
whose statements, promises, answers
are of doubtful integrity

My ghost who travels in a ramshackle conveyance,
who defers indefinitely the embrace
I ask of her

My ghost who moves like lightning
in wide extended flashes
I will one day smash you in many bright empty pieces
    of frost
or at least pare off a thin cold slice of you

Shall send you below the horizon,
turn you back to odds and ends,
make you less than loose fragments of rock
on a steep slope,
an illegible and torn letter
and not my ghost

But not yet
Like the white bird against the dark sky,
you must still move against my life

A repatriation, not a haunting . . .
Ghost putting me to rights again.

Eric Millward

I THINK MY MOTHER NEVER KNEW

I think my mother never knew,
Through all their shared and tender years,
What made my father lie awake,
Or half of what the man went through;
Except that all his private fears
Were borne for someone else's sake.

It was no fault of hers: he kept
To himself whatever plagued him; so
Lying awake at night was just
His chance to work things out. If he slept
Or not, he never let her know.
His silence she would take on trust.

Why did he do it? I think I see
The way he saw it: something about
If you have problems, only you
Can find out where the balm might be;
And if you still can't work things out
There's no use asking others to.

I suppose in this moaning age
A man might be described as quaint
Who shouldered trouble silently.
But I respect my heritage,
In which no self-absorbed complaint
Could ever conquer dignity.

Perhaps he was the loser; though
Leaving us all in health could be
Enough to make the man content.
And it would please him could he know
His wife, alone, sleeps easily,
And lives on what he might have spent.

Frances Bellerby

SLOUCHING ON MY WAY

Slouching on my way,
senseless, and unknown
as unknowing, I came
on a curious scene.

It was a dancing stoat
in the blazing sun
bounding with wildest grace
– partner unseen.

For partner in that dance
existed, I knew,
halting dead in my tracks
– and my heart halted too.

Ecstasy? Terror?
What, in heaven's name
or hell's, had the interloper
unwittingly become?

That empowered dancer,
in a twisting leap,
had made me the partner
– the other might escape.

Where then my status?
My immortal soul?
Fled to the rabbit in the hedge
as it away did crawl?

Whilst all around
in the silent afternoon
furze-pods cracked.
And the dance went on.

On still, and on,
towards some appointed end
where love and terror fuse
and death come with a bound.

Patric Dickinson

NOAH'S DOVE

There in front of my feet
Crossed the black shadow
Of Noah's dove homing
With nothing in its beak
Never to find the Ark.

I stood still as I could
On the turning world.
I forgot where to go,
To home to.
Above the sky was clear,

The full sun shone;
There wasn't a dove in it,
Only I had to move
My shadow somewhere on
Towards the dark.

Derwent May

SIGNS OF FEELING

One man in a large room: writing.
A bus passes, a manhole clinks; and then
The night rubs down to silence again.
Sleep billows out from the children's room: inviting.

He sits on in the large room: waiting.
He casts around for signs of feeling; and then
Abruptly writes a line or two again.
He remembers seeing another sign: hating.

Roger Garfitt

TAEDIUM VITAE

The old man at the window
has no hands. On every row
the clock drops a stitch.
Slowly, with perfect pitch,
a soprano melts in flame.

The exiles draw another game.
Their last finger of gin
stands poured for one of them to win.
Good manners are preventing 'mate.
They do not see the gin evaporate.

Philip Larkin

THE LIFE WITH A HOLE IN IT

When I throw back my head and howl
People (women mostly) say
But you've always done what you want,
You always get your own way
– A perfectly vile and foul
Inversion of all that's been.
What the old ratbags mean
Is I've never done what I don't.

So the shit in the shuttered château
Who does his five hundred words
Then parts out the rest of the day
Between bathing and booze and birds
Is far off as ever, but so
Is that spectacled schoolteaching sod
(Six kids, and the wife in pod,
And her parents coming to stay) . . .

Life is an immobile, locked,
Three-handed struggle between
Your wants, the world's for you, and (worse)
The unbeatable slow machine
That brings what you'll get. Blocked,
They strain round a hollow stasis
Of havings-to, fear, faces.
Days sift down it constantly. Years.

Gavin Ewart

YORKSHIREMEN IN PUB GARDENS

As they sit there, happily drinking,
their strokes, cancers and so forth are not in their minds.
Indeed, what earthly good would thinking
about the future (which is Death) do? Each summer finds
beer in their hands in big pint glasses.
And so their leisure passes.

Perhaps the older ones allow some inkling
into their thoughts. Being hauled, as a kid, upstairs to bed
screaming for a teddy or a tinkling
musical box, against their will. Each Joe or Fred
wants longer with the life and lasses.
And so their time passes.

Second childhood; and 'Come in, number 80!'
shouts inexorably the man in charge of the boating pool.
When you're called you must go, matey,
so don't complain, keep it all calm and cool,
there's masses of time yet, masses, masses . . .
And so their life passes.

LONELINESS

The empty hand has no help nor hold.
Always the fingers fret with clever things,
but the palm aches to close over one shape –
a shoulder perhaps, or familiar contour
of crested hip, or the waist's snug valley –
but these are absent. Nothing takes their place.
Only the stray cat, stiff-legged and mewing,
thrusts its hard head with desperate passion
into the least caress: the hand retreats,
arched and echoing. Easier to cup firelight,
or a full glass, than another hunger.
What was a nest once, nursing precious things,
or could smooth away sweat, or abstract pain
from a sudden hurt, is now an imprint
of its own emptiness. Leaves in autumn
lulled in the still park reflect the pale sun
that peoples the benches in ones and twos,
and talk is halting and inconsequent,
a cortège of unspoken memories,
a marking-time until the frost comes in
and stray cats grow thinner on the ground
and all return stiffly to empty rooms.

James Berry

LUCY'S LETTER

Things harness me here. I long
for we labrish bad. Doors
not fixed open here.
No Leela either. No Cousin
Lil, Miss Lottie or Bro'-Uncle.
Dayclean doesn' have cockcrowin'.
Midmornin' doesn' bring
Cousin-Maa with her naseberry tray.
Afternoon doesn' give a ragged
Manwell, strung with fish
like bright leaves. Seven days
play same note in London, chile.
But Leela, money-rustle regular.

Mi dear, I don' laugh now,
not'n' like we thunder claps
in darkness on verandah.
I turned a battery hen
in 'lectric light, day an' night.
No mood can touch one
mango season back at Yard.
At least though I did start
evening school once.
An' doctors free, chile.

London isn' like we
village dirt road, you know
Leela: it a parish
of a pasture-lan' what
grown crisscross streets,
an' they lie down to my door.
But I lock myself in.
I carry keys everywhere.
Life here's no open summer,
girl. But Sat'day mornin' don'

find mi han' dry, don' find my face
a heavy cloud over the man.

An' though he still have
a weekend mind for bat'n'ball
he wash a dirty dish now, mi dear.
It sweet him I on the Pill.
We get money for holidays.
But there's no sun-hot
to enjoy cool breeze.

Leela, I really a sponge
you know, for traffic noise,
for work noise, for halfway
intentions, for halfway smiles,
for clockwatchin' an' col' weather.
I hope you don't think I gone
too fat when we meet.
I booked up to come an' soak
the children in daylight.

labrish – A Jamaican word: to talk and to gossip without restraint.
naseberry tray – Seller's tray of naseberries, a sweet brown Caribbean
   fruit the size of a small apple.

Alexis Lykiard

SIGNS OF A STRUGGLE

Treacle-black the Stockholm tar
creeps slick and slow down inch-thick
trunks, oozing over each clear scar

where kitten's rapid claws have scratched
white climbing-holds. This oily stuff
painted on, plus new wire netting,

with a bit of luck might do the trick.
So much for growing pains. Apple trees
like young children must also be watched,

need care, attention, safety, all of these
simply to survive. But what's the betting?
Wound succeeds wound: no shield is quite enough

Roger Woddis

THE HERO
(*After 'Wandering Aengus', by W. B. Yeats*)

I went out to the city streets,
Because a fire was in my head,
And saw the people passing by,
And wished the youngest of them dead,
And twisted by a bitter past,
And poisoned by a cold despair,
I found at last a resting-place
And left my hatred ticking there.

When I was fleeing from the night
And sweating in my room again,
I heard the old futilities
Exploding like a cry of pain;
But horror, should it touch the heart,
Would freeze my hand upon the fuse,
And I must shed no tears for those
Who merely have a life to lose.

Though I am sick with murdering,
Though killing is my native land,
I will find out where death has gone,
And kiss his lips and take his hand;
And hide among the withered grass,
And pluck, till love and life are done,
The shrivelled apples of the moon,
The cankered apples of the sun.

This poem was written after the Birmingham bomb outrage of November
21, 1974.

Georgina Hammick

A VIEW OF THE TROUBLES

We're all proud of Andrew who,
At seventeen, got away
From the tractor our village school
Fits boys for, to let the Air Force
Train him as a chef.

Home on leave he shows the rest
Of the lads up, with his clipped
Head and white smile in a tanned
Face – like those posters proclaiming
'It's a Man's Life'. It is, he says.

He drives a car now, and on Sundays walks
Through Sheepwood arm in arm
With a girl who is not local.
He has the glamour of an officer.

I met his mother in the shop last week.
She says that Andrew's off to Belfast soon.
Where he may lose some of that tan. That grin.

Andrew Waterman

AN ULSTER GARLAND

Close by my kitchen window juts
a wall, rich-textured, scarred
brickwork of ochre, grey and red
many times cemented, showing
faint whitewash from before
the house was last patched up.
And where the roof of split slates slopes
to its corner has somehow taken
root among fissures a sprig
of wallflowers, arching
luminous now in the late sunshine.

Delicate, the flowers
have survived nights, and many downpours,
found sustenance amid crumbling.
I have come to expect them.

No, they would not, should it come,
prevail against bulldozer, or bomb;
nor admit their relevance.
And should these petals be torn by explosion,
buried deep under rubble, so
each unique thing must be lost, and is
irrevocable; yet always

others continue, reappear
contriving such root somewhere, so
configured on moving skies.

I drop my gaze on close
unfocused roofline ridges set
at jarring angles.

                    This
is Ireland now, where mobs command
and kill, and terror grips.
'The power system is at breakdown point.'

Lightless, I look
again for the yellow flowers upon
their brink; also remark
among the streets' cross-hatching sprays
of answering greenery, deepening
as day ebbs; in low
untended yards, how cranesbill, vetch,
sweetrocket, speedwell, flowers
run wild I have no name for,
sustain their points of colour; and grass
persists, unorganized. By kind
pervasive to outlast
what coming darkness.

D. J. Enright

THE PROGRESS OF PRYING

It was while living in Nice
That she began the diaries called
'The Nice Diaries'.

Now that 'The Nasty Diaries'
Have been discovered
In an attic in Norfolk
We know what 'Nice' means.

We know of course what 'Nasty' means.
Although her penmanship is so bad
That editors have not yet established
A definitive text,
We know that 'Nasty'
Is not a lake in Finland.

Floods of light are about to be cast
Where hitherto there was no darkness.

Nigel Lewis

HANGMAN'S FIELD

Mushrooms testify
to an underworld,
they sprout from there
in the dark, spore-laden
nose-cones –
mushrooms in skimpy white
skin shirts,
their gills the air-vents
of rocket-engines
ageing like nipples
from pink to deep brown

Unlit candles
ensconced in
underworld
in fairy circles,
pink and white
babies, born blind
in darkness

Collapsing into nothing
within the day
or filling the punnets
of the early morning
mushroom pickers

Who seem ghostlike,
bowing, lowering
their heads in the mist
of the water-meadow
between the two great oaks.

Edmond Leo Wright

FROM *THE HORWICH HENNETS:*
NUMBER 358

Pressed my face in the snow. If I closed one eye,
saw me as solid, not hollow. Struck me how
very funny it was that, if I could spy
from inside, I'd be hollow too. If I could
be a little man, hid inside, I'd see how
my head fitted my school cap, how my skin hood
kept me in, how my eyes were little saucers
to be filled, how my tongue was a kind of sack
you could stuff with words. Lips were rubber borders
you could stretch to make air go buzz, bang and smack
just as they did. Would my looking at them show
just the same, their face pressed into the soft snow?

Wes Magee

THE DEATH ATTICS

In twenty years or more I've discovered three.
One, in Ireland, was a closed barn's frowzy loft
where La's cat had crept to die in a straw bed.
It in turn became bed for a tide of maggots
which crested and broke across its flesh and fur,
and this I trod on, foot anchored in horror
while ghost odours squirmed beneath the dry rafters.

Then, while stowing old trunks in a house attic,
found a bird's shrunken frame, wire legs drawn up tight,
its weight in my hand no more than a feather.
A missing tile was the trap door it fell through
and how it must have panicked till its heart burst
never learning where the sun had gone or why
the sky was ribbed with struts and grown dismal black.

Most recent, an ancient farmstead in Norfolk,
where rat bones littered a loft like hieroglyphs,
the remains of a phosphorous candle killing.
Numerous as match-sticks spilled from a box
they snapped underfoot, fragile and marrowless,
yet holding still that age-old message of fear,
the slick rat biting deep into memory's neck.

Those death attics, the empty heads of houses,
where creatures came to die in dust and darkness
while we blundered far below in pleasant rooms.
Clambering to them now, cursing a skinned shin
and coughing like a yahoo, I shudder at
the thought, find pieces of *my* past, boxed remains,
books, school reports, snaps, golf balls, a worn out shoe.

BRINGING TO LIGHT

powder, chunks of road, twisted
skeletal metal, clay
                         I think
of ancient cities of bringing to light
foundations under the foundations

bringing a raft of tiny
cellars to light of day.
Gold pocks in the
broad sunlight, craters
like a honeycomb bared

*   *   *

In one cellar, a certain mannekin
terribly confined
in his sweat and beard
went crazy as Bosworth.
In another, his jailer lived,
here are his shelves for
cup and smock. He was a jailer
so knew he was free.

*   *   *

Every day the luminous tiers
of the city are filmed with a dust
a light silt from foot and flesh
and the travelling mind.

*   *   *

I have forgotten a picnic on a hill
in Kent when I was six, but
have a page of snapshots about it.
It still takes place, but in
a cellar I cannot locate.

There is a cellar, a cell, a cellular
room where a handsome spirit
of wilfulness picnics with me
all day limber imaginary brother
dandling me between his feet
kissing my eyes and mouth
and genitals making me
all his own all day
                as he is mine.

          *   *   *

But beneath the superior cellars
others reach downward
                      floor under
floor Babel reversed

Opening doors I discover
the debris of sorcery interrupted
    bone structures like experiments

fewer and fewer
joining each other in their origins

separate words return to their roots
lover and mother melt into
one figure that covers its face
nameless and inescapable

need arrayed like a cause

Achilles and Achelous the rivergod
he fought unite in person
and in name as the earlier
Achelous who precedes both

tress of the Greek's hair
                          red-glinting
braids with thick riverweed
the cell darkens with braiding
toward their common root
in the lowest the last the
first cavern, dark and moist
of which
          the foundations
are merely the Earth

        *   *   *

nothing
        but a faint
smell, mushroomy, thin,
as if something, even here,
were separating from its dam
a separating
            of cells

Seamus Heaney

VIKING DUBLIN: TRIAL PIECES

I

It could be a jaw-bone
or a rib or a portion cut
from something sturdier:
anyhow, a small outline

was incised, a cage
or trellis to conjure in.
Like a child's tongue
following the toils

of his calligraphy,
like an eel swallowed
in a basket of eels,
the line amazes itself

eluding the hand
that fed it,
a bill in flight,
a swimming nostril.

II

These are trial pieces,
the craft's mystery
improvised on bone:
foliage, bestiaries,

interlacings elaborate
as the netted routes
of ancestry and trade.
That have to be

magnified on display
so that the nostril
is a migrant prow
sniffing the Liffey,

swanning it up to the ford,
dissembling itself
in antler combs, bone pins,
coins, weights, scale-pans.

III
Like a long sword
sheathed in its moisting
burial clays,
the keel struck fast

in the slip of the bank,
its clinker-built hull
spined and plosive
as *Dublin*.

Now we reach in
for shards of the vertebrae,
the ribs of hurdle,
the mother-wet caches –

and for this trial piece
incised by a child,
a longship, a buoyant
migrant line.

IV
That enters my longhand,
turns cursive, unscarfing
a zoomorphic wake,
a worm of thought

I follow into the mud.
I am Hamlet the Dane,
skull-handler, parablist,
smeller of rot

in the state, infused
with its poisons,
pinioned by ghosts
and affections,

murders and pieties,
coming to consciousness
by jumping in graves,
dithering, blathering.

V
Come fly with me,
come sniff the wind
with the expertise
of the Vikings –

neighbourly, scoretaking
killers, haggers

and hagglers, gombeen-men,
hoarders of grudges and gain.

With a butcher's aplomb
they spread out your lungs
and made you warm wings
for your shoulders.

Old fathers, be with us.
Old cunning assessors
of feuds and of sites
for ambush or town.

VI
'Did you ever hear tell',
said Jimmy Farrell,
'of the skull they have
in the city of Dublin?

White skulls and black skulls
and yellow skulls, and some
with full teeth, and some
haven't only but one'.

and compounded history
in the pan of 'an old Dane,
maybe, was drowned
in the Flood.'

My words lick around
cobbled quays, go hunting
lightly as pampooties
over the skull-capped ground.

Ted Walker

VIPERS

Vipers,

sliding, pour themselves through themselves,
bits of miniature rivers.

Slack else, still
as worry beads left where they fell,

they abrade the young year's sun
in grit, green, brick, stucco brown,

a crumble. Always the eyes, coppery red –
sometimes the tongue, loose threads

flickering the wind.
This one I found

dead today, coils in a coil,
fills its Chinese bowl

with spent resilience. I'll keep it
as long as this takes to write.

Never before did I own a viper. Touch,
flinch,

to remember dry heaths of boyhood
summer, brackens, the sandy birchwood,

yelping in a pack for the hated snake –
deadlyadder. With a fork-ended stick

you'd fix his wriggling, knife his
sin. It was the lore of boys:

make a belt of his skin, heat
the flesh in an iron pan for the fat

that cures deafness.
Older, with a first girl in the sharp, dark grass,

you listened for the swift sibilance
of adders, appalled; and appalled in the silence

after, still you'd listen.
But, since, you've seen them often,

commonplace on an afternoon path,
exotic, arcane, tempting as death

to disturb. Several, zigzagged, ravelled as whips
lashed round themselves, whirls and loops,

finally subsided, a muddled tie-drawer.
One, disentangling, sloughed like a whore

peeling a stocking back. The new
head, mint as a pebble damped with dew,

had to be smashed. This one that's mine,
stiff in its small blood, its venom mine

for the simple milking, could kill
from posthumous spite. Did Adam, some residual

innocence left him in his great age,
lift the serpent's carcass in homage

to the nighthawk?
In the garden, to the dark

under the rose arbor, I commit this thing,
watched from the window. The fang

feels like red wire. I'd have
let this one live.

Stanley Cook

PIGEON COTES ON PENISTONE ROAD, SHEFFIELD

Past where a complex of multi-storey flats
Fences off the view from terraced houses
And above Weir Head where, jammed on stones,
The larger rubbish cordons off the smaller rubbish
From the lower river, a dozen pigeon cotes
Painted football colours stand in clearings
Among the willow herb. This Sunday morning
The pigeons, tethered by instinct and safe in the valley
As a match between cupped hands from the wind,
Crisscross their wings on the air. I remember my Father's
Fostering homers beaten down by a storm
And Uncle Tom's being turbaned with glory
From winning the Federation from San Sebastian.
Sometimes to someone pigeon fanciers,
Backyard mechanics, rabbit breeders,
Hermit chrysanthemum growers on allotments
And trumpet players in silver prize bands
Are/were/will be great.

I. A. Richards

ANGLERS

Upon these banks in peace they sit
Well wrapt, close sheltered from the breeze
That blurs their waters' images;
They alone know what cares they've quit,
Designedly aloof, and tranquilly,
Silently, watching their lives float by.

Now, as they will, may they speculate:
So may they catch (so caught) the FISH
That could consume their every wish.
Within that deepening gloom may lurk
The more-than-Pike whose ancient power
Shall all that swims in time devour;
The wolf that, circling near, will sweep
In as the doom of all their sheep:
Their minutes, counted ere they hatch.

Or fable how, though none know whence.
Another Angler may let fall
Some secret Hook, hid in what bait
Inviting all. There let it wait.
Who gulps it down, who dares to snatch,
Aloft he goes without recall,
Departed hence to none know where.

You cunning ones, with your sly gear,
You but enact through your pretence
The all but universal fate,
O, anglers all, frequenting here.

Yet most, may sanity aver,
Who fish are as intent upon
Endearing duck, patrolling swan,
Willows every breath will stir,
Quietude deaf ear can hear:
Solacings though the turmoil near.

Hugh MacDiarmid

THE DAY BEFORE THE TWELFTH
(Caretaker of Highland Shooting Lodge loquitur)

In come sic a rangel o' gentles
Wi a lithry o hanyiel slyps at their tail
That the hoose in a weaven is gaen
Like a Muckle Fair sale.

Ye canna hear day nor door
For their tongues a' hung i' the middle
Like han'-bells: an' ilk ane squekin an squealin'
Like a doited fiddle!

I wish that the season was owre
Afore it's begun: an the haill jing-bang
Awa' Sooth again: an the hurley hoose
Like a deid man's sang.

Like a deid man's sang i' the white birch wud,
A lanely sang in a toom domain,
While the wutherin' heather lies on the warl'
Like an auld bluid-stain!

rangel o' gentles: lot of gentry folk
lithry o' hanyiel slyps: following of lackeys
hoose in a weaven: house in a hullabaloo
doited: crazy
a':   all

Michael Hamburger

CAT, AGING

Her years measure mine.
So finely set in her ways,
She divines, she sniffs out
Every change in the house,
In the weather, and marks it for me
Though with a flick of an ear
Only a twitch of her tail.
She foretells convolutions,
Departure, thunderstorm,
By not being there – hiding
Behind the heater. At times
She will play yet, kittenish,
Or hunt; but then gathers
All movement, vanity
Into her great stillness
That contains the whole of herself
And more, of her kind. When she stays there,
Dies, it is me she'll prove mortal.

Alan Bold

A HISTORY OF SILK

Climbing through a month-long tunnel
Of metamorphosis
To grow from wormy grub to grubby worm
This skilful creature,
Having eaten the leaves of the
                                    mulberry tree,
Longs to have wings
For a few long-spun-out days of life,
Wings to go mating with.
Taking delicate pains to protect its wings
It spins hundreds of yards of thread
Around itself and then,
When it is almost ready to emerge
And expand its wings outside its cocoon,
It is carefully lifted by the silkmaker
Who admired its monumental handiwork
Who drowns it in hot water
Who assembles its silky spinning
With the efforts of other silkworms.
Later
Some women wear
Expensive hand-painted silk
Next to their sensuous flesh
While they sit over tea
Engrossed in conversation.

John Ormond

DESIGN FOR A QUILT

First let there be a tree, roots taking ground
In bleached and soft blue fabric.
Into the well-aired sky branches extend
Only to bend away from the turned-back
Edge of linen where day's horizons end;

Branches symmetrical, not over-flaunting
Their leaves (let ordinary swansdown
Be their lining), which in the summertime
Will lie lightly upon her, the girl
This quilt's for, this object of designing;

But such, too, when deep frosts veneer
Or winds prise at the slates above her,
Or snows lie in the yard in a black sulk,
That the embroidered cover, couched
And applied with pennants of green silk,

Will still be warm enough that should she stir
To draw a further foliage about her
The encouraged shoots will quicken
And, at her breathing, midnight's spring
Can know new season as they thicken.

Feather-stitch on every bough
A bird, one neat French-knot its eye,
To sing a silent night-long lullaby
And not disturb her or disbud her.
See that the entwining motives run

In and about themselves to bring
To bed the sheens and mossy lawns of Eden;
For I would have a perfect thing
To echo if not equal Paradise
As garden for her true temptation:

So that in future times, recalling
The pleasures of past falling, she'll bequeath it
To one or other of the line,
Bearing her name or mine,
With luck I'll help her make beneath it.

Jane Wilson

MAGGIE'S FLOWER PICTURE

When cold strips the bone
Of any comfort, our duffle-coated Maggie
Is up in her attic, re-organizing June

From between the folds of old newspapers
Where wafers of windflower, asphodel, alyssum
Stay headlines from the pitch of confrontation.

She lifts the flowers and lays them on satin.
Under the compass of her fingers they sprawl and nestle;
Themselves and more in her companionable pattern.

She arranges them, not as they cropped up
In waste plots whispering within earshot
Of sudden light appalled by dust

But as bunting and trumpets amazing the route
To some unexpected reception: a beckoning back
Into the arms of those who were reduced.

Galaxies of hedge-parsley jet
From the full-stop of a paragraph of obituaries;
Roses are pink-skinned yet.

Stanley Cook

A GUY

Burglar alarming to find a man in the hall:
I prove to my spitting nerves it is only the guy
The children have made, sitting dry upon
The sewing machine and leaning against the wall.

Not surprising that in my trousers and shirt
He looks like me; I have a sneaking fear
He will take my place with my wife and children,
Hiding from them he has a newspaper heart.

Strange as seeing the back of one's head
In a tailor's mirror: today when he needs
My alias most it feels uncomfortable
To insist it is he who is already dead.

Outside are gathered the truthful branches of trees
As naked and alike as love or death
And on the ground, potato-crisp curled beneath them,
Lie the abandoned evasions of fallen leaves.

He has gone in my place; the fireworks start
And gardens grow foggy with bonfire smoke:
He lolls in the stink of blistering old lino;
His smouldering stitching gives; he falls apart.

FIREBUG

He's tired of winding up the gramophone
Half way through 'Three Little Maids',
And waiting for a rickshaw to return from the bazaar.
The monsoon teems on the compound.
A coolie, splitting cocoanuts on an iron spike,
Stoops to wring the rain out of his loin-cloth.
The boy picks up a box of matches.

His little sister comes from the nursery holding a doll.
'Give me that!' 'What for?'
'I want to set it on fire.' 'You wouldn't dare.'
'I will if you help me.'
She puts the doll on the floor. He strikes a match
And holds it gingerly under the pink legs.
The girl screeches like a cockatoo.

The fire bursts into song,
Eats the doll, sticks out its tongue, stands up
Gyrating like a crimson top: then dies.
Burnt celluloid leaves a guilty smell.
The girl cries over the ashes, 'Give me back my doll!'
'An angel took it to heaven, didn't you see?'
The devil needs thrashing with a shoe.

John Mole

THE TOY PIANO

The mouth of the toy piano
grits its teeth. It bites
habitually on mice and teddy-bears
but is dissatisfied.

The wired belly tinkles
for stronger meat,
those harmonies of suffering
beyond the cradle.

Branches of dark forests
where each bird has earned its song
enchant the piano;
only what hurts matters

and this child will matter
when he is not a child.
But while they play together
in a lighted room

the piano hates him.

John Hewitt

THE MILE LONG STREET

The mile long street you trudge to school,
past factory wall and painted sills,
house-doors, curtains, little shops,
that padlocked church with lettered board,
was staged and starred with asterisks.
First, harness-shop that flashed with brass,
bits, stirrups, bridles, whips and reins,
huge blinkers for shy animals,
round its door, the leather smells;
farther, under a large sign
which spelt that strange word Farrier,
an open gateway offered you
hammer on anvil, the sharp taste
of scorched horn hissing;
and, farther still, a narrow door,
with glint of straw, warm tang of hay,
scatter of grains fanned round the step
brought the flapping pigeons down.

If you were rich and had a mind
to buy yourself a little horse,
he could be saddled, shod and fed,
and never need to leave that street.

Kingsley Amis

FESTIVAL NOTEBOOK

CLOSING SCENES of the Salisbury Festival:
Haydn and Mozart in St Edmund's Church,
A building soon to be deconsecrated
Because irrelevant to civic needs
And turned into a meaningful hotel.
Involuntarily the mind throws up
Fancies of Japanese, back from Stonehenge,
Quaffing keg bitter by the pulpit stair,
Swedes booking coach-tours in the chancel.

SALISBURY becomes a part of Area 5
In 1974, and so its mayor,
Whose office dates back to 1611
(The year of the King James Bible, actually),
Will soon be as irrelevant as the church,
But need not be turned into anything.

LATER THAT NIGHT, outside the City Hall,
Past the Cadena, Debenham's, Joyland,
Men of the 1st Bn. the Royal Scots
Perform the historic ceremony of Tattoo.
Plaids, bonnets, flash of tenor-drummers' sticks,
The pipes, stir the blood unmeaningfully
Till 'Jesus Christ, Superstar' rings out
In the quick march, and relevance is restored.

Edmond Leo Wright

FROM *THE HORWICH HENNETS:* NUMBER 148

There were notices everywhere. By the spring,
by the shore of the lake, on dams. 'Liverpool
Corporation. Anyone found tampering . . .
tipping filth, waste, or rubbish . . .' Locked in cages,
inside coffers, in tunnels, set with bascule
weights, controlled by chained wheels, and checked by
     gauges
shut in chapels of stone on green mounds, thrusting
water rushed through pipes for the city to drink.
I could hear underground a thrumming. Rusting
slabs and cobbles, dried slime, white grass, and a stink
from the rainbow mud, lay in the overflow.
How I longed for flood! How would the water go?

Tom Lowenstein

THE GUARDIANS AGAINST
TRANSFORMATION

In middle 16th century, spring-time,
Breckland (northern Suffolk),
between Mildenhall and Brandon,
here's a woman (watched by 15 village children),
running across common-land, chasing
(shamelessly, in keeping with her class) a goat.
And shouting words of a strong flavour,
makes a jump at him, boots flying,
falls on his tail, and having fastened herself to him,
takes his coarse beard in her red fist
(dropping the tail) and lugs Billy
through the rough grass, merds and gorse-bushes,
(his face hauled forward, and his back legs dragging,
eyes like yellow onions), and pegs him
onto Mistress Johnson's nanny-goat.
'To it, now!' she murmurs. 'Make a back there for her!'
And the 15 village children watch all afternoon,
the tense legs rearing firmly, trembling . . .
Then comes back the woman with a short stick,
and shouts across the field,
and they grab him by the hard legs and the hair,
and 15 of them pull and pull, and off comes Billy,
with his big thing sticking through his thick coat,
shining like a lance. 'Shall we take 'im to the Grange
for Mistress Pugh, Ma'am?' shout the children.
'What's 'at you say-ee?' 'To do 'er nannies, Ma'am.'
'Oh, aye,' she calls back, 'but mind 'e boards
naught but she-goats there . . . I reck not
what unnatural monsters 'e'd beget in 's heat,
the devil,' she engages to her sister Johnson,
who has arrived to supper the exhausted Nan . . .
a conceit that 15 children never before heard,
as they kick him through the sheep-fold
and the oak-wood where the pigs are eating.

But some, that knew to listen,
remembered themselves marvellously
of frightful prodigies that had been balladed:
of horned and hairy chickens that did bleat
and butt with their coxcombs violently against men's legs.
And so minding themselves to see the office
of some twenty nuptials properly performed,
they did stay till midnight, and not depart
until that hour had passed: and each did get
some small ale, and some pieces of stiff Suffolk cheese
from Mistress Pugh for his attendance there.

Isa Weidman

OUR VILLAGE

Do they think
they've got something extra
these new villagers?

with that extra way
they have of speaking,
sealing their exclusiveness;

what's in their collective head?

Forming the village society
with acceptable ideals – yes,
until they calculate
then strongly feel it hits them;

their plea for
low priced houses
for younger
villagers holds good

until the council's threat
of their proximity;

'Coal in bath' is out,
not yet
'swarms of kids' though
with the pill and that
they'll hammer other finds
some true for all;

Welcome their nice work on
tree preservation
open footpaths, dogs
and their excrement
and the compiling of
a history of our village

with inhabitants
with broad accents
in small houses.

Hugh MacDiarmid

THE AULD HOUFF

The Houff that stood here's
Vanished drap and drain
I'd leifer a' else
In creation had gane,

And let us sit on,
A pack o' auld scamps,
Smokin' like chimlies
And drinkin' like lamps.

The glint o' the whisky
'Ud ha'e ser'd us for licht
And the blue reek hidden
The lack o' ocht else frae oor sicht.

Wha's unbiggit the Houff,
And left – the sun, is't? or mune?
Lichtin' the world like a toom pipe
When the last fill's dune?

houff: old inn
leifer: rather
unbiggit: unbuilt
toom: empty

Wes Magee

ALL NIGHT DISCO

Against
knife like lights my eyes peel like ripe plums
and the white strobe is timed to make you vomit.
Death sounds shriek and squeal to the wild, bucking floor,
amoebas of paint coagulate on walls
and, yes, we move on the bed of some rank pond.

The girls
joggle bodies in isolation
faces white as cut loaves, fingernails purpled
as if they've plundered damsons in the Ladies.
Disorientation's the pain of the game
and as a torture room this takes some beating.

The men,
sidling like weary hunters, stalk flesh
while I grip a drink and cling to the swamped bar.
Cosmic with noise the ceiling aches to faint
as someone flops from a chair like a wet sack.
The groovers, stoned with sound, lurch towards dawn.

Outside
the night's hard dreams
fall to the streets
as rain.

Edwin Morgan

THREE POEMS FROM *THE NEW DIVAN*

Hafiz, old nightingale, what fires there have been
in the groves, white dust, wretchedness,
how could you ever get your song together?
Someone stands by your tomb, thinks
as a shadow thinks: much, little, any?
You swore you'd be found shrouded in another
grave-cloth of pure smoke from a heart as
burning dead as beating, but the names
of cinders are thick where passions were.
Whole cities could be ash. But
not the song the Sufi says we have
but our dying song, you knew, gives us our beings.

*

Swish the incense everywhere it's not.
I know you're full of arak and danger,
a fiery flying dressing-gown on human
wheels, two joss-sticks tossing the lust of
the nose up out through our small world
into the jasmine-banks that smelt before
incense was made. You're in your blood.
Is it like this the gods are,
making and breaking as they swirl? who
box universes like eggs, and on reflection
unbox a cracked one for the pan, when
sparks only as they die are heard.

*

It was a slow caravan accompanied
by dust-devils, a dry thunder journey
to the desert's end. At sight of the forest
indignant camels trod in crevices,
held back puffing. Soon it was dark
under cedars, with more dark to come.
A bundle of lightning dropped badly
down the bark, hurt no one. Has
nature no symbols? They carried
nature like a peacock into the undergrowth
and ate it. Then these
servants of God lay down, each with his
book, in the black covert, by his beast.

Peter Porter

THE DESCENT INTO AVERNUS

Coming down from the serious hills upon
The Campanian flatlands, then we saw
The black lake where the stars reflected shone
Among the stagnant argosies of weed,
Small sulphur roses knocking at the shore
And swollen pumice jammed among the reeds.

This was the Leader's promise, a lake without
Birds or any living creature, fanned
By volcanic breath, the home of doubt;
Here we would camp and wait until a sign
Gave presence to the statutory land,
Blood from the earth or voices in a vine.

One of our purposes was to trace the smell,
That all-pervading smell of misery,
Some said it was the heroes dead in Hell
Smothered forever in their victims' flesh,
Others the pus of gods, rot in the Tree
Of Life no mortal creature could refresh.

That it was human where nothing human lived
Was everyone's hypothesis. The shades of armies
Stood behind the midday dazzle, sieved
From a glut of contours by the sun –
Beyond the line of salt some spindly trees
Waved like souls whose torment had begun.

The Leader made survival rules for all –
To be observers of the scene was our
Responsibility. In the long haul
To darkness, man would need supplies,
Rations which the dead could not devour,
Signals beyond his rational faculties.

And so upon the poisoned earth we sat,
The air itself a teeming oracle:
Man's soul might leave him like a cat,
His body come to carbon, yet somewhere
Behind this valley or that thin-lipped hill
He'd find his true and disciplined despair.

Ted Hughes

SIX POEMS

These six poems are part of a new sequence by Ted Hughes called 'Lumb's Remains'.

I
In the M5 Restaurant
Our sad coats assemble at the counter

The tyre face pasty
The neon of plaster flesh
With little inexplicable eyes
Holding a dish with two buns

Symbolic food
Eaten by symbolic faces
Symbolic eating movements

The road drumming in the wall, drumming in the head

The road going nowhere and everywhere

My freedom
Is to feed my life
Into a carburettor

Petroleum has burned away all
But a still-throbbing column
Of carbon-monoxide and lead.

I attempt a firmer embodiment
With illusory coffee
And a gluey quasi-pie.

2
Before-dawn twilight, a sky dry as talc

The horizons
Bubbling with bird voices

The blackbird arrives a yard away, in a black terror
And explodes off
As if searching for a way out
Of a world it has just been flung into.

The shrews, that have never seen man, are whizzing everywhere.

Who is that tall lady walking on our lawn?

The star in the sky is safe.

The owl on the telegraph pole
Warm and dry and twice his right size
Scratches his ear.

Under the stones are the woodlice, your friends.

3
Let that one shrink into place
Camouflaged and doggo
Under his eye-wall
Like an overlooked lizard.

Let the madman thrash in his pram
And the fool harden his opinion
And the man of bile
Deify his will,

And that one, the eagle-nosed, the broad-handed
Be above the battle – i.e. lie
Carcase under it, cheek turned
To the propitiation of the blow-fly.

Let you keep one world nearer the world
Simple as those puffball rabbits
Who multiply themselves, in abandon and joy

For what seem to be foxes.

McCaig?

4
Stilled at his drink

Old, in his body's deadfall.
His body fills the whole stage.

Spirit has all evaporated
Coolly as alcohol

From the bulbous blue weldings
Of his knuckles, from his whiskery eye-sockets.
Illusion
Cannot raise the energy.

General closure
Has confessed him.

Throat of primordial Iguana
Brain of dried herbs.

He sits – idol of some extinct religion.
The dust worships his feet.

He stares
Into – some wateriness.

Jilted
For the last time.

5
The bulging oak is not as old
As the crooked tree of blood
In the body of the girl
Who marvels at it.

The tree, too, knows its owner.

When she walked away the history oak
That leaned over immortal water
Fell in a flurry of shadows
Ghosting away downstream.

6
Why do you take such nervy shape to become
A victim, so violin-like?

The Inquisitors have caught you.
Now you are under the discretion

Of their fingers and smiles.
'Where do you come from?'

You cannot speak their tongue.
You can only cry wordlessly

Crying sideways
From the eyes of men, to the shut doors

Of the dust-grains. Shaking the dust

Of the wrong world.

Peter Redgrove

TO THOSE WHO CANNOT CATCH
THE DISEASE
(*For Stuart Wilson*)
Let not thy right hand know what thy left hand doeth

I
And we kissed goodbye, and he went one way,
And I went down into the country famous for cheeses,
To its strong dark pear-beers, the pear-honey
So thin and exquisite, shining in its jar
With a pale tinge of blue.

It was not Utopia. There was a Virus.
A limp in the right leg, a shortening in the bones,
A self-digestion, a withering to a dew-claw
High in the groin.

Little pain once the balance was found:
The labyrinths hypertrophic, the great
Semi-circular canals deep in the head;
Perfectly easy to get about one-legged!
Why did I ever need two?

Then the right eye: visions of black lightning
Mining the green fields, and in the night-time
White lightning like star-weld crammed with starheads
Sparking, a glue

Sealing the lid shut on awakening each morning;
Sponging your poor eye, and your left orb
Watches its mate struggling down the drain
Like a dead spider dried in a cave
Withered on strings

But the left eye! What rainbows of vision!
Every bird, he can see its chanting
Like sunlight from each beak
He watches TV without a set,
It flies in full colour across the land;
He sees love everywhere, it is a blue mist,
It is lightning, noiseless:

Thus the afflicted, the sinister cult.
I wanted the great meetings
Of one-legged folk with one shining eye,
Right arms pinned inside their tailcoats,
Chanting with intelligence, left eyes
Ablaze with new broadcasts.

II
Disease? It was a religion!
And there was a Bird
With feathers of fire that stood raving revelation
Invisibly and silently on the wakeful left shoulder.

Many could not become diseased. They joined sadly,
Anxious to perform small tasks, very humbly;
They prepared themselves wistfully to bait the infection,
Adopting an eye-patch, a crutch in the armpit,
A coat with long tails to hide their right legs
Crooked up in a sling, and pinned to the shoulder
A stuffed parrot to stand for the Bird.

The diseased prayed bare-headed.
They had been reborn.
Right sides were placentas.
Real persons were left sides.
Naturally sinister fed on the dexter:
And they told how a new head had grown from their crown,
The child of their left and their right sides in another dimension
The one where God lived
Who had come at night
With a burred whisper lifted the head from the neck
Turned it somehow and put it back.

All healed by the morning.
They spoke of this
In a burr
With a vibrating left tonsil.

The undiseased without revelation wore black hats,
In tricorn, three-dimensional headhouses of the world:
One day would raise it to one who would point, shout
The head! the *other* head! and all would point
And he fling his hat away and stand bare-headed,
Leg shrinking, eye shrinking on its strings in its socket,
Diseased at last and walking one-legged like God,
His friends all pointing, all laughing and pointing!

III
I went down into the country with my sling,
My eyepatch and my three-cornered hat,
My crutch, blue tailcoat all buttoned with silver,
Eager for disease, keen for infection,
All swept and shrived, wooing defilement.

IV
The ghost-town, deserted by Dexters.
In each bolted shop with the shutters up
The material of that trade still plies its trade.

On the shoemaker's bench, a fine left shoe
Cobbles itself out of leather shapes
Stands on a bench, polishes itself glassy,
Rests shining awhile in the falling dust,
Plucks its own nails out and lays itself flat
In the proper drawers, in tanned silence reposes,
Starts cobbling again.

They say if a Sinister is in need
He goes to such towns where the goods keep themselves
At the peak of perfecting, again and again.

Hens gobble their eggs, lay them afresh;
Ham runs squealing to the knife, heals itself;
Looms weave suits, unweave them.

Dexters run the country: honeys, perries,
Pears, wheat, queenbees, asbestos.
Some wait a week, others a lifetime
For the Bird to take them, or the Virus to wither them,
Some cannot catch it. I

Expect there are jobs there. I shall plead for a job.

D. J. Enright

ETERNITY

I can see it now,
Sitting there, next to the Doctor
Listening to Berlioz' '*Damnation*'
Then discussing it at length.

Latini will have something to say
You can be sure
On being ahead of one's time.

Don Juan on Mortuary Art
And the Burden of the Past.
The Old Man's recension of Milton:
Ancient Crux and New Light.

The Case of the Fallen Angel –
Was He Pushed?
A symposium led by Belial.

And the occasional guest speaker.
Jesus on the Harrowing:
Did it Really Work?

There is no end to torments,
The old can be used again and again.
It's in the other place
The programme is a problem.
Heaven help them.

LACHRIMAE

or

Seven tears figured in seven passionate Pavans

Passions I allow, and loves I approve,
only I would wish that men would alter
their object and better their intent.
ST ROBERT SOUTHWELL
'Mary Magdalen's Funeral Tears' 1591.

LACHRIMAE VERAE

Crucified Lord, you swim upon your cross
and never move. Sometimes in dreams of hell
the body moves but moves to no avail
and is at one with that eternal loss.

You are the castaway of drowned remorse,
you are the world's atonement on the hill.
This is your body twisted by our skill
into a patience proper for redress.

I cannot turn aside from what I do;
you cannot turn away from what I am.
You do not dwell in me nor I in you

however much I pander to your name
or answer to your lords of revenue,
surrendering the joys that they condemn.

THE MASQUE OF BLACKNESS

Splendour of life so splendidly contained,
brilliance made bearable. It is the east
light's embodiment, fit to be caressed,
the god Amor with his eyes of diamond,

celestial worldliness on which has dawned
intelligence of angels, Midas' feast,
the stony hunger of the dispossessed
locked into Eden by their own demand.

Self-love, the slavish master of this trade,
conquistador of fashion and remark,
models new heavens in his masquerade,

its images intense with starry work,
until he tires and all that he has made
vanishes in the chaos of the dark.

MARTYRIUM

The Jesus-faced man walking crowned with flies
who swats the roadside grass or glances up
at the streaked gibbet with its birds that swoop,
who scans his breviary while the sweat dries,

fades, now, among the fading tapestries,
brooches of crimson tears where no eyes weep,
a mouth unstitched into a rimless cup,
torn clouds the cauldrons of the martyrs' cries.

Clamorous love, its faint and baffled shout,
its grief that would betray him to our fear,
he suffers for our sake, or does not hear·

above the hiss of shadows on the wheat.
Viaticum transfigures earth's desire
in rising vernicles of summer air.

LACHRIMAE COACTAE

Crucified Lord, however much I burn
to be enamoured of your paradise,
knowing what ceases and what will not cease,
frightened of hell, not knowing where to turn,

I fall between harsh grace and hurtful scorn.
You are the crucified who crucifies,
self-withdrawn even from your own device,
your trim-plugged body, wreath of rakish thorn.

What grips me then, or what does my soul grasp?
If I grasp nothing what is there to break?
You are beyond me, innermost true light,

uttermost exile for no exile's sake,
king of our earth not caring to unclasp
its void embrace, the semblance of your quiet.

PAVANA DOLOROSA

Loves I allow and passions I approve:
Ash-Wednesday feasts, ascetic opulence,
the wincing lute, so real in its pretence,
itself a passion amorous of love.

Self-wounding martyrdom, what joys you have,
true-torn among this fictive consonance,
music's creation of the moveless dance,
the decreation to which all must move.

Self-seeking hunter of forms, there is no end
to such pursuits. None can revoke your cry.
Your silence is an ecstasy of sound

and your nocturnals blaze upon the day.
I founder in desire for things unfound.
I stay amid the things that will not stay.

LACHRIMAE ANTIQUAE NOVAE

Crucified Lord, so naked to the world,
you live unseen within that nakedness,
consigned by proxy to the judas-kiss
of our devotion, bowed beneath the gold,

with re-enactments, penances foretold:
scentings of love amid a wilderness
of retrospection, wild and objectless
longings incarnate in the carnal child.

Beautiful for themselves, the icons fade;
the lions and the hermits disappear.
Triumphalism feasts on empty dread,

fulfilling triumphs of the festal year.
We find you wounded by the token spear.
Dominion is swallowed with your blood.

LACHRIMAE AMANTIS

What is there in my heart that you should sue
so fiercely for its love? What kind of care
brings you as though a stranger to my door
through the long night and in the icy dew

seeking the heart that will not harbour you,
that keeps itself religiously secure?
At this dark solstice filled with frost and fire
your passion's ancient wounds must bleed anew.

So many nights the angel of my house
has fed such urgent comfort through a dream,
whispered 'your lord is coming, he is close'

that I have drowsed half-faithful for a time
bathed in pure tones of promise and remorse:
'tomorrow I shall wake to welcome him.'

John Dowland, 'Lachrimae, or seaven teares figured in seaven Passionate Pavans'; Peter Philips, 'Pavana Dolorosa'; Anon, 'A Cristo Crucificado'; Quevedo, 'En breve carcel . . .'; Lope de Vega, 'Que tengo yo que mi amistad procuras?'.

Pamela Lewis

KARL MARX'S GRAVE

I have always wanted to see
Karl Marx's grave.
I took three kids and a camera
to Highgate Cemetery
on a summer Sunday morning.
I guessed correctly
which side of the road
to look, and asked a sort of gardener
who didn't know anything.
Not a grave digger that one,
nor merry either.
'Must be right,' I said,
'there are foreigners coming
up the path' – it was.
Dear God, I'm glad I wasn't Eleanor
and had to face that granite block
across the breakfast table.
But then, he was not
a larger than life stone bust,
just an extraordinary man.
Certainly that cemetery
is the most neglected
I have seen on either side
of any sea. My children were shocked
to watch me thoughtfully picking
my way back up the paths
by way of the blackberries
bedecking the graves.
'You can't eat those,' they whispered;
'Nonsense,' I said, and it's true,
I'm still alive.

AT JOWETT'S GRAVE

Majestic he sailed,
flagship of a navy,
sails puffed with every wind
that pride could summon.

They were going to *rule*:
to command, to direct, to prescribe,
to categorize, to set in order:

and always with his eye on them.
And damn it, they *did* all those things,
and always with his eye on them,
Never apologize, never explain!
And they never did.

So majestic he sailed
until at last he docked by these flat stones,
got out of his high painted ship, and lay down.

Lay down in sour earth
with nettles, docks and mare's tails
amid the cut-price comforts of small lives
in a graveyard no bigger than a tennis court.

And it is all there today,
for the small lives persist like the mare's tails
(common and beautiful as the veined wings of flies)
and will have their cut-price
comforts and conveniences,
the dock-leaves to assuage their endless nettles:
small pubs, small shops, a factory where they work,
off-licence, fish and chips, a laundromat.

While a few streets away, in the same rooms
where he lived out his life, the port goes round,
the talk goes on, the truths are shredded out
and the points scored, with stroke and counter-stroke
('That was damned bad sherry you gave us, Master,
if it comes to that,' and it does still come to that:)
and he lies in unsunned earth, almost near enough
to catch what they are saying, and join in,
but for the little accident of death.

There is no memorial: I stumbled
on his grave by chance one day,
waiting for my wife to have a baby
in the hospital down the road.
(You were the baby, Toby, and I want
you to accept this poem, if you will –
not that I want you to grow up like Jowett.)

And yet a man could do worse,
worse I mean than grow up like Jowett:
and much, much worse than lie like him in death.

Shaded by the factory wall he lies,
among the docks and nettles and mare's tails:
his navy sunk, his ship burnt long ago:

a candidate for elegy, but not
for pity (who would dare? preposterous!)
One feels his presence there, still (somehow) confident:

secure in the overhead flights of swans
that force the hissing air through their heavy pinions:
in the embrace of earth, the nearness of water,
the cheerful stubbornness of the springing weeds –

still not apologizing, never explaining.

IN 1870

Troppmann was twenty
when cut off before his prime,
that's to say guillotined,
massacre his crime.

Eight persons (in a field at Pantin
hastily interred) his tally.
An entire Alsatian family
bloodily deprived of life.
Butchering Kinck the bore,
that self-made man's meek wife,
their brood of Ovaltineys,
got our bitter werewolf nowhere.

Lethal banality, sullen inventions in the dock:
the Empire crumbled alongside Jean-Baptiste.

Other more talented exiles
guessed the wild longings, caged
horizons of deceitful Cain.
Both Lautréamont the youth's contemporary
and Bolitho over half a century
later, kept his name green as bile.

Failure's absurd logic, to kill for gain!
Troppmann's trapped now in the amber
of what unwittingly he wanted
much too fast – not money but style.

Thomas Blackburn

MENTAL WARD

They shall be new as the roots of their sane trees
After the various drugs to ward off disaster.
They shall drift down like birds from the high fells
To the limbs of the trees where no one is a stranger.

They shall celebrate their union with each other,
Men and women, speechless in life, dumb as the roots of trees,
In good communion of talk and laughter
And prove they are found now who had lost their ways.

For these are those who in the parish of living
Having no good instrument on which to play,
Still worked hard and with the almost nothing
Of their scant tongue and brain on the great symphony.

The man who barked like a dog shall talk of angels.
The girl, so far gone no skill could disinter
Her buried soul, in superb parabolas
Of dance and song celebrate the life in her.

O there shall be no more desolation or crying anywhere there.

For the great pianist who strummed on one string
With a broken finger, shall have an infinity of chords,
And the stopped poet who could only say 'Good morning',
Reap with his tongue a harvest of meaningful words.

They shall be written in the middle of the page
Who were in parenthesis here,
For withdrawn from the body that held them in close siege
There shall be no more desolation anywhere.

No more desolation anywhere.

Kit Wright

VERSIONS OF DR TYERLEY

(Dr Tyerley practised in a Victorian mental hospital and believed in the psychotherapeutic value of cricket.)

(1) A PLAYER TO THE LUNCHEON GUESTS

I was a bowler for Dr Tyerley's team
 That played another of this name
Lately, on the Doctor's grounds. You came,
 You remember, by the privet gate
  To the field's edge that day
  To see the madmen play –
And the Doctor's Burgundy and haunch of pork
Slurred in your bellies as rich talk
  Of Hunt and Steam and State
  Gave, down the orchard, way
   To a white gleam
Of us odd fellows dancing the Doctor's dream.

But I was a bowler for Dr Tyerley's side
 Against another – his men too –
And the first trick of all was mine to do:
 Bowl the first ball, begin the game.
  I tell you this is so:
  I could not let it go.
I ran up to the stumps. Then shied. Stopped.
Three times I tried. And stuck. So I was dropped
  From the Doctor's side. The shame
  Killed me when I came
   To the tree where he tied
My arms and legs and left me. I'm a wide.

(2) A PLAYER TO THE DOCTOR

Fat Dr Tyerley
  Sweatily scrabbled:
Played the game hard.
Charged round the yard
Like a bull in a ring,
Booming us on
For the game was the thing
To make a man well:

Dear Dr Tyerley,
How could you tell?

Fat Dr Tyerley
  Grovelled and grappled:
Hurled the burst ball
At the stump-painted wall,
Cranked the chipped bat
That was gone in the spring,
Thundered *How's that?*
At a wicket laid low:

Sweet Dr Tyerley,
How should we know?

Fat Dr Tyerley
  Mightily struggled:
Rearing and clouting,
Praising and shouting
Over the scrum
In the exercise yard
Of the wailing and dumb
Advice and abuse:

Kind Dr Tyerley,
What was the use?

Much, Dr Tyerley.
   Sadly we straggled:
I and the rest,
Players long past our best,
Kept, mortally, error
That lay beyond games,
But who, from locked terror,
First gave me the key?

You, Dr Tyerley,
Playing for me.

James Berry

FOLK ADVICE

Call tiger Master
  it will still eat you

Sugar cane doesn't grow
  like grass

Cow that belongs to a butcher
  never says 'I'm very well'

Fox preaches
  to take care of the lamb

An obeah man's daughter
  is always pretty

Never call alligator long-mouth
  till you pass him

Watch your story too
Long story will make other man catch
    runaway black man

Never pull out your insides
  and give them to a stranger
   then take dry leaves and stuff yourself

Trouble never blows conch shell
  when it's coming

When trouble catches a man
  a little girl's frock will fit him

You shake hands
  you don't shake hearts

When you see everybody else running
  you take time

obeah : Caribbean word for witchcraft

THE CONTRIBUTORS

DANNIE ABSE was born in Cardiff in 1923. He has published six books of poems, of which the most recent is *Funland*, two novels, *Ash on a Young Man's Sleeve* (1954) and *O. Jones, O. Jones* (1970) and a volume of autobiography, *A Poet in the Family* (1974). Several of his plays have been published and performed, and he has also edited the poetry series, Modern Poets in Focus.

FLEUR ADCOCK was born in Papakura, New Zealand, in 1934. She was educated at numerous schools in England and New Zealand and at Victoria University of Wellington, N.Z., where she read classics. Since 1963 she has been settled in London and works as a librarian in the Foreign and Commonwealth Office. Her publications include *Tigers* (1967), *High Tide in the Garden* (1971), and *The Scenic Route* (1974), all published by Oxford University Press.

KINGSLEY AMIS was born in 1922 in Clapham. Educated at the City of London School and St John's College, Oxford. He is married to the novelist Elizabeth Jane Howard. He has taught at four universities, finally retiring in 1963, and has published some twenty-one books, of which three are collections of verse.

PAT ARROWSMITH is 45 and lives with another lesbian. She was educated at Stover School, Cheltenham Ladies' College, Cambridge University (B.A. History), Ohio University and Liverpool University (Social Science Certificate). She is a Pacifist Socialist and belongs to War Resisters' International, C.N.D., T.G.W.U., Troops Out Movement and British Withdrawal from N. Ireland Campaign. She has had numerous odd jobs in cafés, hospitals, offices, council parks etc and has been a Local Authority social caseworker. For over ten years she has been a full-time organizer in various branches of the peace movement. A political prisoner nine times, she was twice adopted by Amnesty International. Her published works include *Jericho* (novel – Cresset Press); *Somewhere Like This* (novel – W. H. Allen and Panther); *To Asia in Peace* (non-fiction – Sidgwick and Jackson); *The Colour of Six Schools* (non-fiction – Soc. of Friends Race Relations Committee); *Breakout* (poems and drawings from prison – Edinburgh University Student Publications Board). She also paints in water colours and has had work exhibited in London Borough festivals, theatre foyers etc. Pat Arrowsmith now works in the secretariat of Amnesty International.

FRANCES BELLERBY: Before her death in August 1975, Frances Bellerby supplied the following note: West Country birth, childhood. Some Welsh blood (mother's side). Deeply affected in schooldays by First World War. Many varied jobs in many varied places – e.g. teaching and games coaching, kennelmaid work, newspaper work, chiefly commissioned topographical articles, dramatic criticism, odd-job reporting, librarian work East End hospital etc. Wrote short stories; three collections and one novel published. Poetry from age of four (or earlier); did not try for publication until in forties. Four books of verse, fifth in press (1975). Writes only verse. Lived in Cornwall intermittently for years, then consistently for thirteen years.

JAMES BERRY was born in a village in Jamaica. He lived four years in America before coming to London. He contributes to the Barbadian literary magazine, *Bim*, and the journal of the Caribbean Artists Movement, *Savacou*, based in Jamaica. His poems have also appeared in *The Listener, London Magazine, Poetry Review, Tribune*, and *Limestone Magazine*. He organized the Jamaica 10th and 12th Independence Anniversary Festival readings. He has published short stories, broadcast some, and had a radio play produced. He has given many broadcast talks on growing up in the West Indies and on race relations. He works full time as a telegraphist.

THOMAS BLACKBURN is the author of seven books of poems (*The Outer Darkness, The Holy Stone, In the Fire, The Next Word, A Smell of Burning, A Breathing Space, The Fourth Man*) and also of several critical works, a novel and a well-known volume of autobiography, *A Clip of Steel*. A keen mountaineer, he is proud of having introduced Christian Bonington to the sport. He works as a lecturer in English at a London college. His 'Selected' Poems have just been published by Hutchinson.

ALAN BOLD, the poet and visual artist, was born in Edinburgh in 1943 and lives there with his wife Alice, and daughter Valentina. He has published a dozen collections of poetry (e.g. *The State of the Nation*, Chatto 1969), has appeared in *Penguin Modern Poets 15* (1969), and has edited *The Penguin Book of Socialist Verse* (1970). He has exhibited paintings, etchings, drawings and illuminated poems and has organized several large exhibitions of figurative painting. Forthcoming books include new poetry, a critical study of *Thom Gunn & Ted Hughes* (Oliver and Boyd), an anthology of *War Poetry* (Pergamon), and *The Cambridge Book of English Verse 1939–75*.

PETER BRENNAN: Born Birmingham 1950. Attended various universities. A few poems published in submerged magazines. Now teaches in London.

ALAN BROWNJOHN was educated at London elementary and grammar schools and Merton College, Oxford. He has taught in several kinds of schools and now lectures in a College of Education. He has published five collections of verse: *The Railings* (Digby Press, 1961), *The Lions' Mouths* (Macmillan, 1967), *Sandgrains on a Tray* (Macmillan, 1969), *Brownjohn's Beasts (for Children)* (Macmillan, 1970) and *Warrior's Career* (Macmillan, 1972). Under the pseudonym John Berrington he published a novel, *To Clear the River* (Heinemann 1964, Penguin 1966). He edited the anthology *New Poems* 1970–71 (with Seamus Heaney and Jon Stallworthy) and *First I Say This* (Hutchinson, 1969). He has published poems, articles and reviews in all the leading journals including *New Statesman, Encounter, Ambit, Observer, London Magazine* etc. His work has frequently been featured on Radio 3, in the 'Poetry Now' series and in individual programmes. In 1972 BBC TV's programme Omnibus, and in 1973, Full House, were concerned with his work.

STANLEY COOK was born in 1922 at Austerfield, a village in South Yorkshire. Read English at Oxford. Taught at schools in Lancashire and Yorkshire. Now lives in Sheffield and lectures in the Department of English Studies at the Polytechnic, Huddersfield. First prize in Cheltenham Festival Poetry Competition, 1972. He has published a sequence in pamphlet form, 'Form Photograph' (1971) and a collection of poems, *Signs of Life* (1972). Married with a son and two daughters.

JOHN COTTON was born in London in 1925. From 1962 to 1972 he was editor of *Priapus*. His collection, *Old Movies and Other Poems*, published by Chatto and Windus, was a Poetry Book Society recommendation and won an Arts Council publication award. His recent collection, *Kilroy Was Here* (Chatto and Windus) was the Poetry Book Society Choice for Spring 1975. He is currently editor of *The Private Library* and has been chairman of the Poetry Society. He lives with his wife and two sons in Berkhamsted. He recently completed a novel.

KEVIN CROSSLEY-HOLLAND was born in 1941. His collection of poems, *The Rain-Giver*, was published by André Deutsch in 1972 and a second collection, *The Dream-House*, is now with the printer. He has translated *Beowulf* and many of the Old English shorter poems and written a book about eight British Islands, *Pieces of Land*, and a number of books for children. His most recent book is *Green Blades Rising*, a study of the Anglo-Saxons in The Mirror of Britain Series of which he is general editor. He is now editorial director at Victor Gollancz Ltd.

PETER DALE: Born, Addlestone, Surrey, 1938; educated: Strode's School Egham, St Peter's College, Oxford. Now Associate Editor of *Agenda*, he has published two books of verse: *The Storms* (1968) and *Mortal Fire* (1970); two books of translation: *Villon* (Macmillan: 1973) and *The Seasons of Cankam* (Agenda Editions: 1975). The University of Ohio Press is publishing his selected poems in Autumn 1975. This book, which contains his latest collection of poems and a verse-play, will also be distributed in England by Agenda Editions.

DONALD DAVIE was born in 1922 and educated at Barnsley Holgate Grammar School and St Catherine's College, Cambridge. He has been a Fellow of Trinity College, Dublin, and of Gonville and Caius College, Cambridge. Since 1968 he has been Professor of English at Stanford University, California. His more recent publications include *Ezra Pound: Poet as Sculptor*, and *Collected Poems, 1950–1970*. His recreations are verse translation, literary politics and travel.

PATRIC DICKINSON was born in Nasirabad, India, in 1914 and educated at St Catherine's College, Cambridge, where he was a Classical Exhibitioner. His poetry publications include, *This Cold Universe, More than Time* and *A Wintering Tree*. Translations: *Complete Plays of Aristophanes* and *The Aeneid of Vergil*. Also *A Durable Fire* a play, *Byron, A Round of Golf Courses*, two anthologies, *Soldier's Verse*, and *Poems to Remember* and an autobiography, *The Good Minute*. With Erica Marx and J. C. Hall he edited the fourth P.E.N. anthology, *New Poems 1955*. He acted as BBC Poetry Editor from 1945 to 1948 and was appointed Gresham Professor in Rhetoric in Gresham College 1964–5. He is married, has a son and daughter, and lives in Rye, Sussex.

PATRICIA DUNCKER was born in Kingston, Jamaica in 1951. Her childhood was spent in the West Indies where her father was a business man and her mother was a teacher. She first came to England in 1964 and was educated at Bedales School and Newnham College,

Cambridge. She is at present working for a doctorate in English and German literature at St Hugh's College, Oxford.

DOUGLAS DUNN was born in 1942 in Renfrewshire. His books are *Terry Street* (Faber, 1969); *The Happier Life* (1972); *Love or Nothing* (1974). He lives in Hull, and works as a freelance writer. He founded Poets' Theatre in 1975, and its first production was his verse play, 'Experience Hotel', performed at the Humberside Theatre in June, 1975.

D. J. ENRIGHT returned to England recently after twenty years of teaching in the East and now works in publishing. Publications include *Memoirs of a Mendicant Professor* (1969), *Selected Poems* (1969), *Shakespeare and the Students* (1970), *Daughters of Earth*, poems (1972), *Man is an Onion* (literary essays) (1972) and *The Terrible Shears*, poems (1973). Another book of poems, *Sad Ires*, is due in the autumn.

GAVIN EWART was born in London in 1916, and educated at Wellington College and Christ's College, Cambridge. He has worked for the British Council and as an advertising copywriter. His first poems were published in *New Verse* in 1933 and his books include *Poems and Songs* (1939), *Londoners* (1964), *Pleasures of the Flesh* (1966), *The Deceptive Grin of the Gravel Porters* (1968) and *The Gavin Ewart Show* (1971). Due this autumn is *Be My Guest!* (Trigram Press). *Penguin Modern Poets No. 25* also includes his work.

ELAINE FEINSTEIN was born in Bootle and brought up in Leicester. She was educated at Newnham College, Cambridge, and since then has read for the bar, worked on the editorial staff of the Cambridge University Press and lectured in the Literature Department of the University of Essex. She is now writing her fifth novel. Her publications include two books of poems, *The Magic Apple Tree* and *The Celebrants*, and she has translated the poems of Tsvetayeva for the Oxford University Press and Penguins. Her novels are *The Circle*, *The Amberstone Exit*, *The Glass Alembic* and *Children of the Rose*. She has also written two television plays, the first of which, *Breath*, was a BBC Play for Today early in 1975. She is married, with three children, and lives in Cambridge.

ROY FULLER was born in 1912. He is a Governor of the BBC and a director of the Woolwich Equitable Building Society. His most recent book is a collection of poems called *From the Joke Shop*. With the late Clifford Dyment and Montagu Slater he edited the first P.E.N. anthology, *New Poems 1952*.

173

ROGER GARFITT was born in 1944, and was educated at Tiffin School, Kingston-upon-Thames, and at Oxford. Now living and writing in North Devon. In 1973 won the Guinness International Poetry Prize at the Stroud Festival. In 1974 received the Gregory Award. First full-length collection *West of Elm* published by Carcanet in 1975. In October takes up a Creative Writing Fellowship at the University College of North Wales, Bangor. Poetry critic of the *London Magazine*.

W. S. GRAHAM was born in Greenock, Scotland in 1918. He has published six books of verse. *Cage Without Grievance*, Parton Press David Archer 1942. *The Seven Journeys*, Maclellan Glasgow 1944. *2ND Poems*, Nicholson and Watson 1945. *The White Threshold*, Faber and Faber 1949. *The Nightfishing*, Faber and Faber 1955. *Malcolm Mooney's Land*, Faber and Faber 1970. His work has appeared widely in this country and in America and Canada. A new book is coming out with Faber next year.

THOM GUNN was born in Gravesend in 1929. He has lived in San Francisco for most of the last twenty years. His last book of poems, *Moly*, was published in 1971. His next, Jack *Straw's Castle and Other Poems*, is due in 1976.

MICHAEL HAMBURGER was born in Berlin in 1924. He emigrated to England in 1933 and was educated at Westminster School and Christ Church, Oxford. Between 1951 and 1964 he lectured in turn at the Universities of London and Reading, resigning a readership in German at Reading in 1964 in order to devote himself to full-time writing. In addition to numerous contributions to literary and scholarly journals, his publications include translations, several critical works and collections of his own poetry. His recent publications are *Ownerless Earth* (new and selected poems), *A Mug's Game*, *Intermittent Memoirs*, *Art as Second Nature* (occasional pieces) and the bilingual anthology *East German Poetry*, all published by Carcanet Press; and *Hofmannsthal: Three Essays* (Princeton University Press).

GEORGINA HAMMICK: Born in 1939 in Hampshire. Educated at boarding schools in England and at Limuru Girl's School, Kenya. Did courses at the Academie Julian, Paris, and Salisbury Art School and afterwards taught at various schools. Has written poetry since childhood, but only recently begun to work seriously and to send poems out. At present working with her twin sister on a picture book for children. Is married to Charles Hammick, bookseller. They have three children and live in Long Sutton, Hampshire.

SEAMUS HEANEY was born in 1939 in County Derry. He worked in Belfast until 1972 when he moved to County Wicklow. His published works include *Death of a Naturalist* (1966), *Door into the Dark* (1969), *Wintering Out* (1972) and *North* (1975). In 1973 he received the American–Irish Foundation's Literary Award.

JOHN HEWISH was born in Polruan, near Fowey, Cornwall, in 1921. After school he studied aircraft engineering. He spent a peaceful Second World War on naval aerodromes, and then read English at Oxford. He has had various jobs, including teaching and journalism, but hardly a career. Since 1968 he has worked in the British Library in London. He has written a study of Emily Brontë.

JOHN HEWITT was born in Belfast in 1907. He has been the Deputy Director of the Belfast Museum and Art Gallery and was also the Art Director of the Herbert Gallery Museum, Coventry. His *Collected Poems 1932–67* was published by MacGibbon and Kee in 1968. His latest book of poems, *Out of My Time: Poems 1967–74* was published by the Blackstaff Press, Belfast, in 1974.

GEOFFREY HILL: Born 1932 in Bromsgrove, Worcs. Educated County High School, Bromsgrove, Keble College, Oxford. Elected a Fellow of the Royal Society of Literature, 1972. Literary Awards include the Hawthornden Prize and the Geoffrey Faber Memorial Prize. Volumes of poetry: *For the Unfallen* (1959), *King Log* (1968), *Mercian Hymns* (1971), *Somewhere Is Such a Kingdom: Poems 1952–1971* (U.S.A., 1975).

MOLLY HOLDEN was born in 1927 and now lives in the West Midlands with her husband and two children. She was severely disabled by multiple sclerosis in 1964. She has a research M.A. from King's College, London. Her published books of poetry include *To Make Me Grieve* (1968) also *Air and Chill Earth* (1971), the Poetry Book Society Recommendation for 1971. She won the Arts Council Award in 1969 and the Cholmondeley Award for Poems in 1972. She has also published novels for older children which include *The Unfinished Feud* (1970), *A Tenancy of Flint* (1971), and *White Rose and Wanderer* (1972). Another novel, *Reivers' Weather*, was published in 1973 and *the Country Over* (poetry) in 1975. She has had poems published also in *The Times Literary Supplement*, the *Review*, the *New Review*, the *New Statesman*, the *Listener*, and other P.E.N. anthologies. She has also had poems read on BBC-Radio and BBC-2 Television, and has published some literary criticism.

TED HUGHES was born in Mytholmroyd, West Yorkshire, in 1930, and from Mexborough Grammar School went to Pembroke College, Cambridge. His publications include *The Hawk in the Rain* (1957), *Lupercal* (1960), *Meet My Folks!* (1961), *The Earth-Owl and Other Moon People* (1963), *How The Whale Became* (1963), *Nessie the Mannerless Monster* (1964), *Woodwo* (1976), *Poetry in the Making* (1968), *The Iron Man* and *Crow* (1970). He was married to the late Sylvia Plath, and now lives in Devonshire with his second wife Carol and his two children.

ELIZABETH JENNINGS was born in Lincolnshire in 1926, educated at Oxford High School and St Anne's College, Oxford. She was Assistant Librarian in Oxford City Library from 1950 to 1958 and later worked as editorial assistant at Chatto and Windus. Her first book of poems won an Arts Council Prize, and her second the Somerset Maugham Award in 1956. She was co-editor with Dannie Abse and Stephen Spender of the fifth P.E.N. anthology in 1956. Other books of poems include *The Mind Has Mountains* (1966), *Collected Poems* (1967), *The Animals, Arrival* (1968), *Lucidities* (1970), *Relationships* (1972) and a book of poems for children, *The Secret Brother* (1966). Most recent publication, *Growing Points* (1975). She has a forthcoming critical book, *Seven Men of Vision*, due in 1976.

JENNY JOSEPH: Born in 1932. Scholar of St Hilda's College, Oxford, reading English 1950–53. Worked on newspapers and spent some time in Southern Africa in the late 50s. Has mostly lived in London since 1959. Her first book of poetry, *The Unlooked-for Season*, published in 1960 was followed by three children and six children's books. This first book received a Gregory award. In January 1975 Dent's published her collection, *Rose in the Afternoon*, and in July 1975 she received a Cholmondeley award. She is currently occupied with a project concerning children and poetry, a book for foreigners learning English, a book of stories; and poetry.

R. D. LANCASTER was born in London in 1922. Among the periodicals his poems have been printed in are: *Essays in Criticism, The Listener, London Magazine, New Statesman, The Observer, New Blackfriars, The Times Literary Supplement*. 'To Karen' is the last poem in an unpublished sequence, 'Mixed Education'.

PHILIP LARKIN was born in 1922. Has published novels and poems, the most recent volume being *High Windows* (1974). Was awarded the Queen's Gold Medal for Poetry in 1965, and made CBE in 1975. Is currently Librarian of the University of Hull.

LAURENCE LERNER was born in Cape Town in 1925, and educated at the University of Cape Town and Pembroke College, Cambridge. He has taught English at the University of Ghana and Queen's University, Belfast, and more briefly in Dijon, various American universities and Munich, where 'The Beech in the Park' was written; he is now at the University of Sussex. His publications include *The Englishman* (a novel), *The Truest Poetry* (a critical work), and four books of poetry, *Domestic Interior* (1959), *The Directions of Memory* (1964), *Selves* (1969) and A.R.T.H.U.R. (1974). Further publications consist of a second novel, *A Free Man* (1968) and three further books of criticism, *The Truthtellers* (1967), *The Uses of Nostalgia* (1972) and *Introduction to English Poetry* (1975). He has recently won the Prudence Farmer Poetry Prize.

NIGEL LEWIS is twenty-seven, and works as a freelance journalist. He was educated at Midhurst Grammar School and Magdalene College, Cambridge. He was born in British Honduras, now Belize, and is working on a novel set in that part of the world. Among his favourite poets are Gary Snyder, Ted Hughes, and Vladimir Holan.

PAMELA LEWIS was born in Nottingham; trained as an Occupational Therapist in London; is married with three children and lives in her hometown. Her first collection *One Mile From The Centre* was published by Turret Books, 1971.

Her poems have been broadcast on BBC Radio 3 and 4 and on Northern Drift, and have been included in the anthologies *Shapes and Creatures* by Geoffrey Grigson and *Impetus* (Ginn & Co.). Published in *Cornhill*, *Encounter*, *English*, *The Magazine*, *I.C.A.*, *Omens*, *Poetry Review*, *Samphire*, *Workshop* and other little magazines.

TOM LOWENSTEIN. Born near London, 1941, attended Cambridge, on and off, 1960–5. Between 1967–71 taught at South Hackney School. Compiled a six-volume poetry anthology for non-readers: contracted for, completed, then abandoned in the slump. Taught English, Education and Creative Writing at Northwestern University near Chicago 1971–4. Worked in 1973 at the Alaska State Museum, making learning-materials for Indian and Eskimo schools. At present living in an arctic Eskimo village working on a book of oral/poetic history. Publications: *Our After-fate*, poems, Softly Loudly Books, London, 1971; *Eskimo Poems from Canada and Greenland*, Allison & Busby and University of Pittsburgh Press, 1974; *Mrs Owl and the Field Marshal*, Anvil Press, Spring 1976. A book of pseudo-divination, *Booster*, just completed.

ALEXIS LYKIARD: Born Athens 1940. Educated at Radley and King's College, Cambridge where he read English, graduating with First Class Honours in 1962. He has published six novels (all now Panther paperbacks) including *The Summer Ghosts*, *Strange Alphabet* and *The Stump*; several poetry collections, among them *Robe of Skin*, *Greek Images* and *Lifelines*, and the first complete annotated translation of Lautréamont's *Les Chants de Maldoror* (Allison & Busby). He has also edited selections of ghost stories by Sheridan Le Fanu and E. F. Benson. Since 1970 he has been living in the West Country.

HUGH MACDIARMID is the pseudonym of Christopher Murray Grieve, born August 1892. Author, in addition to many prose books in the fields of biography, topography, politics, and essays in literary and musical appreciation, of over fifteen volumes of poetry. He was the founder of the Scottish Centre of P.E.N., and one of the founders of the Scottish Nationalist Party. For his services to Scottish literature he has been awarded a Civil List Pension by H.M. the Queen, the honorary LL.D. by Edinburgh University, the Foyle Poetry Prize, £1000 special award by the Scottish Arts Council, elected Fellow of the Modern Language Association and appointed Professor of Literature to the Royal Scottish Academy.

WES MAGEE was born in Greenock, Scotland in 1939. At present working as a Junior School teacher in Swindon; and as winner of New Poets Award for 1972 his first volume *Urban Gorilla* was published by Leeds University Press. Previously he was included in Faber & Faber's *Poetry Introduction: 2*. Also writes short stories, and is working on a novel for children.

DEREK MAHON was born in Belfast in 1941 and educated at Belfast schools and Trinity College, Dublin. He spent a year each in Canada and the United States and taught for a further three years in Ireland before moving to London in 1970, since when he has worked as a free-lance writer. He was 1975 Henfield Writing Fellow at the University of East Anglia and now lives in Surrey with his wife and son. He has published three collections: *Night-Crossing* (1968), *Lives* (1972), and *The Snow Party* (1975).

PAUL MATTHEWS was born in 1944. He is married with two children. He gained an English degree at Sussex University and while studying in Brighton he worked with George Dowden and edited *11th Finger* with Paul Evans. Later he trained in the Rudolf Steiner education methods at Emerson College in Sussex, where at present he is teaching experimental writing. He gives poetry readings, and his work has appeared widely in magazines and anthologies, including *Children of Albion* (Penguin), and *C'mon Everybody* (Corgi). Several booklets of his poetry have been published. 'Rocking-Chair' is due to appear in a booklet of his poems called *Verge*.

DERWENT MAY, who was born in 1930, is the literary editor of *The Listener*. He was the co-editor, with James Price, of *Oxford Poetry 1952*, and is the author of three novels, *The Professionals* (1964), *Dear Parson* (1969) and *The Laughter in Djakarta* (1973). He is married, with a son and a daughter, and lives in Regent's Park.

ALEC McCOLM: Born Glasgow 1920. Educated Colston's School Bristol and Worcester College, Oxford (Open Exhibition in English but read P.P.E.). War Service in Royal Signals, India and Burma. Career in industrial management (soap, light clothing, garden business, contracting, etc.) and management selection consultancy terminated by stroke 1970. Formerly played rugby, squash, the violin and a fairy in *Iolanthe*. Mountaineer 1947–52. Two daughters with and two sons by first marriage 1951. Collects 19th century watercolours. Divorced and remarried 1972. One cat.

ERIC MILLWARD: Born March, 1935, in Longnor, Stafford-shire, the son of a farmer, and educated at Buxton College, Derbyshire, Published in many magazines, including *The Listener*, *The Poetry Review*, *Tribune* and *Outposts*, and in many anthologies, here and abroad; also broadcast by BBC and SABC. Was Poetry Editor of *Towards Survival* until that journal folded. Founder-member of The Conservation Society in the hope of saving mankind from itself. Has since wondered (often) if it is *worth* saving: any fresh evidence of love reminds him it is, perhaps. Has compiled *Earthwords*, an environmental anthology which will probably never reach print – likewise a collection of his own work. Spends rather too much time despising 'tame' (or Establishment) experts – lawyers, politicians, planners, etc – and bad poets, and feeling compasssion for helpless minorities, including *good* poets. Will probably end up writing 'for posterity', if any. Has two young sons, for whom he would preserve even our imperfect society and has recently happily remarried. Now lives in Horsham, Sussex.

JOHN MOLE was born in 1941, brought up in Somerset, and now lives in Hertfordshire where he writes, teaches and is an editor for the Mandeville Press, Hitchin. He is married with two sons. His poetry has appeared in many periodicals and his books include *The Love Horse* (Peterloo Poets) 1973; and *A Partial Light* (Dent); 1975.

EDWIN MORGAN was born in Glasgow in 1920 and is a present Titular Professor of English at Glasgow Univeristy. His publications include *The Vision of Cathkin Braes* (MacLellan, 1952), *The Cape of Good Hope* (Peter Russell, The Pound Press, 1955), *Gnomes* (Akros Publications, Preston, 1968), *The Second Life* (Edinburgh University Press, 1968), *Twelve Songs* (Castlelaw Press, 1970), *Glasgow Sonnets* (Castlelaw Press, 1972), *Instamatic Poems* (Ian McKelvie, 1972), *From Glasgow to Saturn* (Carcanet Press, 1973), a Poetry Book Society Choice, and *Essays* (Carcanet Press, 1974), (as translator) *Beowulf* (Hand & Flower Press, reprinted by University of California Press, 1962), (as translator) *Poems from Eugenio Montale* (University of Reading School of Art, 1959), *Wi the Haill Voice: 25 Poems by Vladimir Mayakovsky* (Carcanet Press, 1972); (as editor) *Collins Albatross Book of Longer Poems* (Collins, 1963). A selection of Edwin Morgan's work is included in *Penguin Modern Poets 15*.

RICHARD MURPHY lives on the west coast of Ireland. He is the author of *Sailing to an Island*, *The Battle of Aughrim* and *High Island*. Recently he has been teaching at Princeton.

JOHN ORMOND was born in Dunvant, Glamorgan, in 1923. Educated at Swansea Grammar School and University College, Swansea, he was a staff writer for *Picture Post* from 1945–9. Since 1955 he has been a documentary film-maker with the BBC. A selection of his work appeared in the Corgi *Modern Poets in Focus* series and a further selection is to appear in *Penguin Modern Poets* next year. His books *Requiem and Celebration* (Christopher Davies, 1969) and *Definition of a Waterfall* (Oxford University Press, 1973) won major Welsh Arts Council Literature Prizes, and in 1975 Ormond received the Cholmondeley Award.

PETER PORTER was born in 1929 in Brisbane, Australia, and brought up in that sub-tropical city. He was educated at local public schools and has had various jobs – newspaper reporter, warehouseman, clerk, bookseller's assistant and advertising writer. He now lives in London and works as a freelance writer. His books of poems include *Once Bitten, Twice Bitten* (1961), *Poems Ancient and Modern* (1964), *A Porter Folio* (1969) and *The Last of England* (1970). *Preaching to the Converted* and *After Martial* were published in 1972. He edited *New Poems 1971–72*.

KATHLEEN RAINE was born in 1908 and educated at Girton College, Cambridge. Her most recent publications include *Faces of Day and Night* (1973), *Farewell Happy Fields* (autobiography, 1973),

The Land Unknown (autobiography, 1975), *The Lost Country* (poetry 1972) and *On a Deserted Shore* (poetry, 1973).

PETER REDGROVE is widely published and anthologized, and teaches at the Falmouth School of Art. His seven books of verse include *Dr. Faust's Sea-Spiral Spirit* (Routledge, 1972) and *The Hermaphrodite Album* (with Penelope Shuttle: Fuller D'Arch Smith, 1973). He has also published a poem-novel called *In the Country of the Skin* (Routledge), which won the Guardian Fiction Prize for 1973. He is represented in *Penguin Modern Poets XI* and was co-editor of *New Poems 1967*. His selected poems of 20 years *Sons of my Skin* (edited by Marie Peel) came out in 1975 from Routledge, and in 1974 he published a novel of mystery and the occult, *The Terrors of Dr Treviles*, co-authored with Penelope Shuttle, which was the subject of a BBC TV film on *Second House*. His radio script of *In the Country of the Skin* won a Writers' Guild Nomination, and his second full-length radio play *The God of Glass* is due for broadcast in 1976. A third novel *The Glass Cottage* is scheduled for publication by Routledge early in 1976, as is a volume of *Selected Drama* from Calder and Boyars. A further volume of new poems *Ogre Yoga* is also in preparation, and he is writing a non-fiction work with Penelope Shuttle on the psychology of the feminine mooncycle. Peter Redgrove read Science at Cambridge and has worked as visiting poet to Buffalo University N.Y., Gregory Fellow in Poetry at Leeds University, and Professor of Literature at Colgate University N.Y., and was a pupil of the psychologist and anthropologist John Layard.

HENRY REED, the poet, critic and radio dramatist, was born in 1914 and educated at Birmingham University. His poetry publications include *A Map of Verona* (1946), and *Lessons of the War*, and he has also written *The Novel Since 1939*.

I. A. RICHARDS, born 1893, in Cheshire. Took to philosophy 1911 at Magdalene College, Cambridge, and to teaching for the English Tripos 1919–39. Wrote with C. K. Ogden *The Meaning of Meaning* (1920–2), and with James Wood and Ogden *The Foundations of Aesthetics* (1922). Then many books by himself. Took to verse with *A Leak in the Universe* (Playbook, New Directions 1958). Then *Goodbye Earth* (1958); *The Screens* (1960); *Tomorrow Morning, Faustus* (1962); collected verse, *Internal Colloquies* (Harcourt Brace Jovanovich 1965); much verse since. In prose *Beyond*, 1974, *Poetries, Their Media and Ends* (Monton 1975), *Complementarities* (Harvard University Press and Carcanet 1976).

VERNON SCANNELL was born in 1922. Freelance writer. Most recent publications: *The Tiger and the Rose*, an autobiography (Hamish Hamilton), Selected Poems (Allison & Busby) and *The Winter Man*, a new collection of poems (Allison & Busby), *The Apple Road*: poems for children (Chatto and Windus). *Not Without Glory*, a critical book on British and American poetry of the Second World War (The Woburn Press), and a collection of poems, *The Loving Game* (Robson Books) are due in 1975.

PETER SCUPHAM was born in Liverpool in 1933 and educated at St George's, Harpenden, and Emmanuel College, Cambridge. He is married with four children and teaches in Hertfordshire. He has published *The Small Containers* (Phoenix Pamphlet Poets, 1972), *The Snowing Globe* (Peterloo Poets, 1972), and *The Gift* (Keepsake Press, 1973). His latest book is *Prehistories* (O.U.P. 1975). He is the founder and co-editor, with John Mole, of The Mandeville Press, a private press for the publication of new poetry.

PENELOPE SHUTTLE was born near London in 1947. Three novels have appeared from Calder & Boyars: *An Excusable Vengeance*, 1967; *All the Usual Hours of Sleeping*, 1969; and *Wailing Monkey Embracing a Tree*, 1974. A fourth novel will appear from Calder & Boyars in 1976, *Rainsplitter in the Zodiac Garden*. She has collaborated with Peter Redgrove on two recent books: *The Hermaphrodite Album*, poems, Fuller d'Arch Smith, 1973; and *The Terrors of Dr Treviles*, a novel, Routledge & Kegan Paul, 1974. Her poetry has appeared in the following collections: *Nostalgia Neurosis* (St Alberts Press), *Midwinter Mandala* (Headland Publications), *Photographs of Persephone* (Quarto Press), *Autumn Piano* (Rondo Publications), and *The Songbook of the Snow* (a holograph collection, from Janus Press). Forthcoming poetry includes *Webs on Fire* (Gallery Press) and *The Dream* (Sceptre Press). She has received two Arts Council Grants, in 1969, and in 1972. In 1972 she won the Greenwood Poetry Prize. In 1974 she received an E. C. Gregory Award for Poetry. Her radio play *The Girl Who Lost Her Glove* was joint third prize winner in the Radio Times Drama Bursaries Competition 1974, and this play was broadcast on Radio 3 in March 1975. Work in progress includes a novel, *The Mirror of the Giant*; a radio play, *The Dauntless Girl*, and, with Peter Redgrove, a non-fiction work on the feminine moon-cycle. Penelope Shuttle lives in Cornwall.

C. H. SISSON was born in Bristol, 1914, and educated at the University of Bristol and in France and Germany. Wasted many years in the Civil Service and a few in the army. He now lives in Somerset, and has written novels, critical works, translations and a book on public administration. *In the Trojan Ditch* (collected poems and selected translations) was published by Carcanet Press in 1974.

GEORGE TARDIOS. Born London 1944. Greek Cypriot parents. Began writing seriously at Secondary school. Expelled aged 18. For six years held numerous jobs including window cleaner, Croupier, Security Guard, Night Club doorman and Public Relations Officer. At twenty-five attended Teacher Training College. Awarded B.Ed. degree 1973. Then offered combined writing scholarship/course managing position at the Arvon Foundation. Married seven years. Now Director of the Foundation's Centre in Devon. Reviewer for S.W. Arts Magazine. Other work appearing in *Lamb and Thundercloud*, poetry anthology edited by Peter Redgrove, and another anthology for teachers of speech and drama edited by Marjorie Lyons (publisher Samuel French).

ANTHONY THWAITE was born in 1930. He has taught in universities in Japan and Libya, worked as a BBC producer, was literary editor of *The Listener* and later of the *New Statesman*, and is now co-editor of *Encounter*. He has published five books of poems, most recently *New Confessions* (Oxford University Press, 1974), and a selection in the Penguin Modern Poets series.

CHARLES TOMLINSON's latest collection of verse is *The Way In* (Oxford University Press). *Renga*, a translation into English of a composite poem by Octavio Paz, Jacques Roubaud, Edoardo Sanguineti and Tomlinson, will appear from Penguin in 1977. An exhibition of paintings, drawings and collages was held in 1972 at Oxford University Press and a second at the Cambridge Poetry Festival in 1975. In the autumn of this year Carcanet Press will publish *Black and White: The Graphics of Charles Tomlinson*, with an introduction by Octavio Paz.

ANNE HAMILTON TURNER was born in Glasgow in 1925, and educated at Whitehill School; now lives in Leeds where she works as a secretary. Married, two sons. Her work has appeared in many periodicals and anthologies, and has been broadcast on Radio Three, Scottish and Northern programmes.

JOHN WAIN has been Professor of Poetry at the University of Oxford since 1973. He has written several novels and works of criticism, and his books of poetry include *A Word Carved on a Sill* (1956), *Weep Before God* (1961), *Wildtrack* (1965), *Letters to Five Artists* (1969), *The Shape of Feng* (1972) and *Feng* (1975).

TED WALKER's publications include *Fox on a Barn Door*, *The Solitaries*, and *The Night Bathers*; and his latest collection of poems, *Gloves to the Hangman* appeared in 1973 from Jonathan Cape. He has received the Eric Gregory Award, the Cholmondeley Award, the Alice Hunt Bartlett Award and a major Arts Council of Great Britain Award. He is currently poet-in-residence at New England College, Arundel. Recently he was made a Fellow of the Royal Society of Literature.

ANDREW WATERMAN was born in 1940 in London, where he lived, and worked at a variety of jobs, until going to university at Leicester and Oxford in his mid-twenties. Since 1968 he has been a lecturer in English at the New University of Ulster, and during this period has been writing and publishing poetry. His first collection, *Living Room*, was published by the Marvell Press in 1974, and was a Poetry Book Society choice.

ISA WEIDMAN. Developing interest in writing poetry since two sons followed their careers. Husband dedicated artist. Very much enjoys living in Kent countryside.

JANE WILSON – born in Hampshire 1923. Educated at Abbots Bromley and Streatham Froebel College. Now living in Leeds, married with 2 sons. She has worked with deprived children, and taken drama in boys' Approved School. Currently teaching Spoken English and Drama at Huddersfield Technical Teachers' Training College. Contributor to P.E.N. Anthology 1973/4, Arts Council New Poetry 1975. York Poetry pamphlet, *Hooligan Canute*, 1974; poetry broadcast in *Poetry Now* and *Poetry Scotland*. Work also broadcast in *The Northern Drift*, *The Sunday Collection*, and *Listen With Mother*. Plays include *A Small Success* broadcast 1975, and *Keep Right On To The End Of The Pier* in commission.

ROGER WODDIS: ex-Customs officer, playwright and regular contributor of satirical verse to the *New Statesman* since 1970. Writes for television, radio, the theatre, short stories, humorous and children's books. Lectures on the writer's craft for ILEA. Television credits include 'That Was The Week That Was', 'The Prisoner', 'Haunted' and Armchair Theatre. Wrote 'A Wilderness of Roses', a play about Margaret Paston, for the BBC-TV series, 'Churchill's People'. Radio credits include 'Conan Doyle Investigates' (radio version of his stage-play produced at the Victoria Theatre, Stoke-on-Trent); 'The Swedish Match', Chekhov adaptation; 'Eugenie Grandet', adaptation of Balzac's novel; 'Morning Story'; and is a regular contributor to 'Week Ending', BBC radio weekly satirical programme.

DAVID WRIGHT was born at Johannesburg in 1920 and educated at Oxford. He has published five books of poems of which the last was *Nerve Ends* (1969), besides several anthologies, including the Penguin *The Mid-Century: English Poetry 1940–1960*, and *Longer Contemporary Poems*, prose translations of *Beowulf* and *The Canterbury Tales*, and (in collaboration with Patrick Swift) three books of travel: *Algarve, Minho and North Portugal*, and *Lisbon*; also an autobiography, *Deafness*. From 1965 to 1967 he was Gregory Fellow in Poetry at the University of Leeds. He is married and lives in the north of England.

KIT WRIGHT. Born 1944 in Kent. Educated at Berkhamsted School and New College Oxford. Taught in a South London Comprehensive, then spent three years lecturing in English Literature at Brock University, Ontario. Since 1970 has been Education Secretary of the Poetry Society. Poetry in Chatto *Treble Poets 1* (with Elizabeth Maslen and Stephen Miller) and *Faber Introduction 3. The Immense Commode* due from the Trouser Press at Christmas 1975. Also writes songs and children's entertainments.

EDMOND LEO WRIGHT, D.Phil. (Oxon.). Head of English Dept., Chipping Norton School (Comprehensive). Papers on literary semantics in philosophical journals. Poems last year in *Encounter, Stand, Phoenix, Samphire, The Little Word Machine*, etc. Sequence *The Horwich Hennets* forthcoming, The Peterloo Press, 1976.